Strangers
at the Gates Again

THE ASIAN AMERICAN EXPERIENCE

Strangers
at the Gates Again

ASIAN AMERICAN
IMMIGRATION AFTER 1965

Ronald Takaki

PROFESSOR OF ETHNIC STUDIES
THE UNIVERSITY OF CALIFORNIA AT BERKELEY

Adapted by Rebecca Stefoff

WITH CAROL TAKAKI

Chelsea House Publishers

New York ❈ Philadelphia

On the cover Hmong women from Southeast Asia pose for the camera before demonstrating traditional dances at the Asian Resettlement Center in Bellevue, Washington in 1985.

Chelsea House Publishers

EDITORIAL DIRECTOR   Richard Rennert
EXECUTIVE MANAGING EDITOR   Karyn Gullen Browne
COPY CHIEF   Robin James
PICTURE EDITOR   Adrian G. Allen
ART DIRECTOR   Robert Mitchell
MANUFACTURING DIRECTOR   Gerald Levine
ASSISTANT ART DIRECTOR   Joan Ferrigno

The Asian American Experience

SENIOR EDITOR   Jake Goldberg
SERIES DESIGN   Marjorie Zaum

Staff for *Strangers at the Gates Again*
EDITORIAL ASSISTANT   Scott D. Briggs
PICTURE RESEARCHER   Ellen Barrett Dudley

Adapted and reprinted from *Strangers from a Different Shore,*
© 1989 by Ronald Takaki, by arrangement with the author and Little, Brown and Company, Inc.

Text © 1995 by Ronald Takaki. All rights reserved.
Printed and bound in the United States of America.

First Printing
1   3   5   7   9   8   6   4   2

Library of Congress Cataloging-in-Publication Data
Takaki, Ronald T., 1939–
   Strangers at the gates again: Asian American immigration after 1965/Ronald Takaki.
         p. cm. — (The Asian American experience)
         Includes bibliographical references and index.
ISBN 0-7910-2190-4.
1. United States—Emigration and immigration—Juvenile literature.
2. Asia—Emigration and immigration—Juvenile literature.
3. Immigrants—United States—Juvenile literature. 4. Asians—United States—Juvenile literature. [1. United States—Emigration and immigration. 2. Asian Americans.] I. Title. II. Series: Asian American experience (New York, N. Y.)
JV6455.T34 1995   94–21105
325'.25'0973—dc20   CIP
                                                                    AC

Contents

On the eve of the second great wave of immigration
from Asia, America's growing multiculturalism was reflected
in many classrooms like this one in Washington State.

AS A CHILD IN HAWAII, I GREW UP IN A MULTICULTURAL corner of America. My own family had roots in Japan and China.

Grandfather Kasuke Okawa arrived in Hawaii in 1866, and my father, Toshio Takaki, came as a 13-year-old boy in 1918. My stepfather, Koon Keu Young, sailed from China to the islands when he was a teenager.

My neighbors were Japanese, Chinese, Hawaiian, Filipino, Portuguese, and Korean. Behind my house, Alice Liu and her friends played the traditional Chinese game of mah-jongg late into the night, the clicking of the tiles lulling me to sleep.

Next to us the Miuras flew billowing and colorful carp kites on Japanese boy's day. I heard voices with different accents, different languages, and saw children of different colors.

Together we went barefoot to school and played games like baseball and *jan ken po*. We spoke "pidgin English," a melodious language of the streets and community. "Hey, da kind tako ono, you know," we would say, combining English, Japanese, and Hawaiian. "This octopus is delicious." Racially and culturally diverse, we all thought of ourselves as Americans.

But we did not know why families representing such an array of nationalities from different shores were living together and sharing their cultures and a common language. Our teachers and textbooks did not explain the diversity of our community or the sources of our unity.

After graduation from high school, I attended a college in a midwestern town where I found myself invited to "dinners for foreign students" sponsored by local churches and clubs like the Rotary. I politely tried to explain to my kind hosts that I was not a "foreign student." My fellow students and even my professors would ask me how long I had been in America and where I had learned to speak English. "In this country," I would reply. And sometimes I would add: "I was born in America, and my family has been here for three generations."

Asian Americans have been here for over 150 years. They are diverse, coming originally from countries such as China, Japan, Korea, the Philippines, India, Vietnam, Laos, and Cambodia. Many of them live in Chinatowns, the colorful streets filled with sidewalk vegetable stands and crowds of people carrying shopping bags; their communities are also called Little Tokyo, Koreatown, and Little Saigon. Asian Americans work in hot kitchens and bus tables in restaurants with elegant names like Jade Pagoda and Bombay Spice. In garment factories, Chinese and Korean women hunch over whirling sewing machines, their babies sleeping nearby on blankets. In the Silicon Valley of California, rows and rows of Vietnamese and Laotian women serve as the eyes and hands of production assembly lines for computer chip industries. Tough Chinese gang members strut on Grant Avenue in San Francisco and Canal Street in New York's Chinatown. In La Crosse, Wisconsin, Hmong refugees from Laos, now dependent on welfare, sit and stare at the snowdrifts outside their windows. Asian American engineers do complex research in the laboratories of the high-technology industries along

Route 128 in Massachusetts. Asian Americans seem to be everywhere on university campuses.

Today, Asian Americans belong to the fastest growing ethnic group in the United States. Kept out of the United States by immigration restriction laws in the 19th and early 20th centuries, Asians have recently been coming again to America. The 1965 immigration act reopened the gates to immigrants from Asia, allowing 20,000 immigrants from each country to enter every year. In the early 1990s, half of all immigrants entering annually are Asian.

The growth of the Asian American population has been dramatic: In 1960, there were only 877,934 Asians in the United States, representing a mere one half of 1% of the American people. Thirty years later, they numbered about seven million, or 3% of the population. They included 1,645,000 Chinese, 1,400,000 Filipinos, 845,000 Japanese, 815,000 Asian Indians, 800,000 Koreans, 614,000 Vietnamese, 150,000 Laotians, 147,000 Cambodians, and 90,000 Hmong. By the year 2000, Asian Americans will probably represent 4% of the total United States population. In California, Asian Americans already make up 10% of the state's inhabitants, compared with 7.5% for African Americans.

Yet very little is known about Asian Americans and their history. Many existing history books give Asian Americans only passing notice—or overlook them entirely. "When one hears Americans tell of the immigrants who built this nation," Congressman Norman Mineta of California observed, "one is often led to believe that all our forebearers came from Europe. When one hears stories about the pioneers going West to shape the land, the Asian immigrant is rarely mentioned."

Indeed, many history books have equated "American" with "white" or "European" in origin. In his prize-winning study, *The Uprooted*, Harvard historian Oscar Handlin presented—to use the book's subtitle—"the Epic Story of the Great Migrations that Made the American People." But Handlin's "epic story" completely left out the "uprooted" from lands across the Pacific Ocean and the "great migrations" from Asia that also helped to make "the American people." As Americans, we have origins in Europe, the Americas, Africa, and also Asia.

We need to include Asians in the history of America. How and why, we ask in this series, were the experiences of these various groups—Chinese, Japanese, Korean, Filipino, Asian Indian, and Southeast Asian—similar to and different from each other? Comparing the experiences of different nationalities can help us see what events were particular to a group and also highlight the experiences they all shared.

Why did Asian immigrants leave everything they knew and loved to come to a strange world so far away? They were "pushed" by hardships in the homelands and "pulled" by demands for their labor in Canada, Brazil, and especially the United States. But what were their own fierce dreams— from the first enterprising Chinese miners of the 1850s in search of "Gold Mountain" to the recent refugees fleeing frantically on helicopters and leaking boats from the ravages of war in Vietnam?

Besides their points of origin, we need to examine the experiences of Asian Americans in different geographical regions, especially Hawaii compared with the mainland. The time of arrival also shaped their lives and communities. About one million people entered the United States between the California gold rush of 1849 and the 1924 immigration act that cut off the flow of peoples from Asian countries. After a break of some 40 years, a second group numbering about four million came between 1965 and 1990. How do we compare the two waves of Asian immigration?

To answer our questions in these volumes, we must study Asian Americans as men and women with minds, wills, and voices. By "voices" we mean their own words and stories as told in their oral histories, conversations, speeches, and songs as well as their own writings—diaries, letters, newspapers, novels, and poems. We need to know the ordinary people.

So much of history has been the story of kings and elites, as if the "little people" were invisible and voiceless. An Asian American told an interviewer: "I am a second-generation Korean American without any achievements in life and I have no education. What is it you want to hear from me? My life is not worth telling to anyone." Similarly, a Chinese immigrant said: "You know, it seems to me there's no use in me telling you all this! I was just a simple worker, a farm worker around here. My story is not going to interest anybody." But others realize they are worthy of attention. "What is it you want to know?" an old Filipino immigrant asked a researcher. "Talk about history. What's that . . . ah, the story of my life . . . and how people lived with each other in my time."

Their stories can enable us to understand Asians as actors in the making of history and as people entitled to dignity. "I hope this survey do a lot of good for Chinese people," a Chinese man told an interviewer from Stanford University in the 1920s. "Make American people realize that Chinese people are humans. I think very few American people really know anything about Chinese." Elderly Asians want the younger generations to know about their experiences. "Our stories should be listened to by many young people," said a 91-year-old retired Japanese plantation laborer. "It's for their sake. We really had a hard time, you know."

The stories of Asian immigrations belong to our country's history. They need to be recorded in our history books, for they reflect the making of America as a nation of immigrants, as a place where men and women came to find a new beginning. At first, many Asian immigrants—probably most of them—saw themselves as sojourners, or temporary migrants. Like many European immigrants such as the Italians and Greeks, they came to America thinking they would be here only a short time. They had left their wives and children behind in their homelands. Their plan was to work here for a few years and then return home with money. But, after their arrival, many found themselves staying. They became settlers instead of remaining sojourners. Bringing their families to their adopted country, they began putting down new roots in America.

But, coming here from Asia, many of America's immigrants found they were not allowed to feel at home in the United States. Even their grandchildren and great-grandchildren still find they are not viewed and accepted as Americans. "We feel that we're a guest in someone else's house," said third generation Ron Wakabayashi, National Director of the Japanese American Citizens League, "that we can never really relax and put our feet on the table."

Behind Wakabayashi's complaint is the question: Why have Asian Americans been considered outsiders? America's immigrants from Pacific shores found they were forced to remain strangers in the new land. Their experiences here were profoundly different from the experiences of European immigrants. Asian immigrants had qualities they could not change or hide—the shape of their eyes, the color of their hair, the complexion of their skin. They were subjected not only to cultural and ethnic prejudice but also to racism. Unlike the Irish and other groups from Europe, Asian immigrants were not treated as individuals but as members of a group with distinctive physical characteristics. Regardless of their personal merits, they sadly discovered, they could not gain acceptance in the larger society.

Unlike European immigrants, Asians were victimized by laws and policies that discriminated on the basis of race. The Chinese Exclusion Act of 1882 barred the Chinese from coming to America because they were Chinese. The National Origins Act of 1924 totally prohibited Japanese immigration.

The laws determined not only who could come to America but also who could become citizens. Decades before Asian immigration began, the United States had already defined the complexion of its citizens: the Naturalization Law of 1790 had specified that naturalized citizenship was to be reserved for "whites." This law remained in effect until 1952. Unlike white ethnic immigrants from countries like Ireland, Asian immigrants were denied citizenship and also the right to vote.

But America also had an opposing tradition and vision, springing from the reality of racial and cultural "diversity." Ours has been, as Walt Whitman celebrated so lyrically, "a teeming Nation of nations" composed of a "vast, surging, hopeful army of workers," a new society where all should be welcomed, "Chinese, Irish, German,—all, all, without exceptions." In the early 20th century, a Japanese immigrant described in poetry a lesson that had been learned by farm laborers of different nationalities—Japanese, Filipino, Mexican, and Asian Indian:

> *People harvesting*
> *Work together unaware*
> *Of racial problems.*

A Filipino immigrant laborer in California expressed a similar hope and understanding. America was, Macario Bulosan told his brother Carlos, "not a land of one race or one class of men" but "a new world" of respect and unconditional opportunities for all who toiled and suffered from oppression, from "the first Indian that offered peace in Manhattan to the last Filipino pea pickers." Asian immigrants came here, as one of them expressed it, searching for "a door into America" and seeking "to build a new life with untried materials." He asked: "Would it be possible for an immigrant like me to become a part of the American dream?"

This series invites students to learn how Asian Americans belong to the larger story of the rich multicultural mosaic called the United States of America.

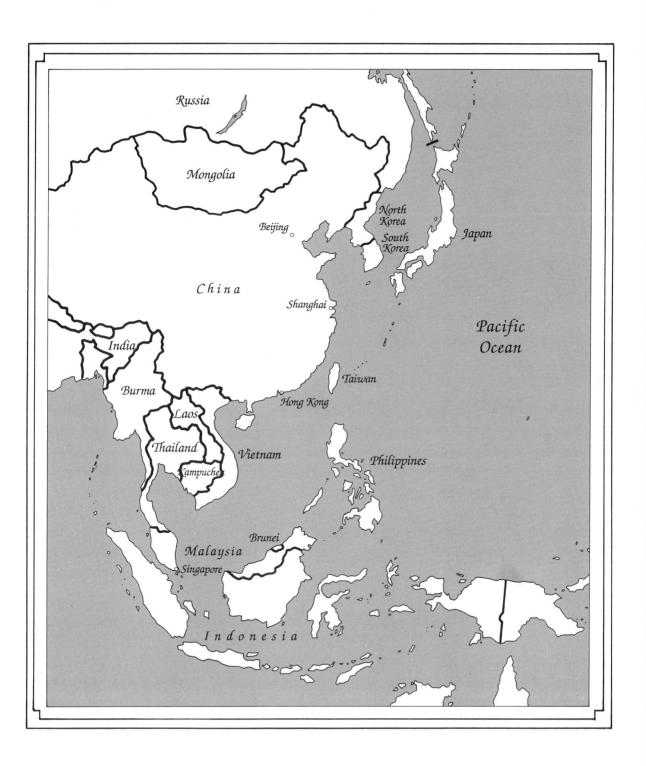

An elderly Japanese American man on his way home from the relocation camp where he spent World War II. The war reshaped the lives of Asian Americans, bringing hardship to some and new opportunities for citizenship to others.

Chapter One

After World War II

IN 1953, A WOMAN NAMED FUSAYO FUKUDA KAYA achieved a goal that had been beyond her reach for more than three decades: She became a citizen of the United States. Born in Japan, she had come to America in 1919 to marry Yokichi Kaya, also an immigrant from Japan. The Kayas worked on a farm in California. They did not own the farm, for state laws prevented Asian immigrants from buying their own land, just as federal law prevented them from becoming U.S. citizens.

The Kaya's family life was torn apart in 1942, soon after the United States went to war against Japan in World War II. The Kayas were among the thousands of Japanese immigrants in America's West Coast states who, along with their American-born children, were rounded up and taken to concentration camps because some Americans—including military and political leaders—charged that they might be secretly loyal to Japan. They lost their homes, their jobs, and most of their possessions. As the war drew to its end in 1945, the Japanese were released from the camps. The Kayas did not return to California because, as their daughter later explained, "Everything they had worked for was gone." Instead, they settled in Arizona.

The Japanese immigrants had received grossly unfair treatment during the war, but as the war ended, the winds of change began to blow across the American landscape. People began to see that American ideals such as fairness and democracy must be applied to all people, regardless of race. To the great joy of those who had come to the United States from Asia, Congress passed a law in 1952 that made them eligible to apply for naturalized citizenship. Fusayo Fukuda Kaya was one of the many Asian immigrants who applied. "She studied hard for the citizenship exam," recalled Kaya's daughter, and

Americans of Japanese ancestry return to Seattle from the Minidoka wartime camp in Idaho. Many of those who had been sent to the camps had nothing to return to, for they had lost their homes, jobs, and businesses.

in 1953, 34 years after she had arrived in America, Kaya proudly stood before a judge and took the oath of U.S. citizenship. She and thousands like her had finally been allowed to claim the United States as their country.

Immigrants from China began arriving in Hawaii and the mainland United States in the mid-19th century. They were followed in the early 20th century by newcomers from other Asian lands: Japan, Korea, the Philippines, and India. But this first wave of Asian immigration aroused alarm among some white Americans, who feared that Asian immigrants would take jobs away from white workers, or that the presence of Asians would mean that the United States could no longer be a "white man's country." In 1924, the U.S. Congress responded to these fears by passing an immigration law that prohibited immigration from Asia. America had slammed its gates shut to Asians. Those who were already in the United States could remain, but they could not bring in their families to join them and they could not become citizens. In addition, many states had laws that kept Asians from owning land or marrying white people.

World War II changed the lives of these Asian immigrants in many ways, some bad and some good. The Japanese American communities on the West Coast were destroyed when the Japanese were sent to the camps under military guard. But the war also blew a fresh breath of democracy through America and opened the way for acceptance of people from Asia.

During the war in Europe, the United States and its allies had fought Nazi Germany, and many Americans had come to see that the Nazis ideas of racial superiority were repulsive. Fighting racism abroad, Americans became more aware of discrimination at home. Notions of white superiority became less popular and less easy to justify. Even before the war ended, President Franklin D. Roosevelt had outlawed racial discrimination in factories that made defense equipment such as airplanes and weapons. In 1947, President Harry Truman created the Committee on Civil Rights to examine the subject of fairness in America.

At the same time, the U.S. courts were also advancing civil rights for racial minorities. For years, laws in many states had prevented intermarriage between people of different races, but in 1948, the California Supreme Court ruled that such laws were against the U.S. Constitution. The court stated that these laws were based on racial distinctions that were "odious

19

to a free people" and did not belong in a country founded upon "the doctrine of equality." That same year, the U.S. Supreme Court put an end to rules that certain communities had established to make sure that only people of certain races could buy homes there. Such rules, said the Supreme Court, were a form of racial discrimination. The courts were beginning to insist that all people, regardless of race, receive equal protection under American laws. Asian Americans, like African Americans, should receive fairer treatment. Although Asian immigrants had come to America from a "different shore" than Europeans, they were protected by the Constitution.

Change was not just handed down by presidents and courts. It also came from the people themselves, from communities across the land. In California, for example, the rights of Asian Americans took an important step forward with changes in the state's land laws. For a long time, people of Asian descent had been unable to own land unless it was registered in the names of their adult American-born children. During the 1940s, the California Justice Department had been enforcing this law and seizing land that it claimed was illegally held by Japanese people. By the end of 1946, California had claimed the property of more than 60 Japanese landowners, including the family of Kajiro and Kohide Oyama. But the Oyamas fought back.

The Oyamas had bought six acres of farmland in San Diego, registering the property in the name of their six-year-old son Fred, who was born in the United States and was a U.S. citizen. The Oyamas were officially the guardians of their son's estate. But in 1944, after the Oyamas had been taken away to a camp with thousands of other Americans of Japanese descent, the state claimed the Oyamas' property, charging they had broken the law that prevented them from owning land. The Oyamas fought the case all the way to the United States Supreme Court, insisting that the land was a gift to their son, who was legally entitled to own it. In 1948, the Supreme Court ruled in favor of the Oyamas and said that California's land law was "nothing more than outright racial discrimination." Said the court, "The only basis for this discrimination

A Japanese American family in 1945, on their recently acquired farm in Louisiana. Such families from the West Coast made new starts in other parts of the country in the postwar years.

against an American citizen was the fact that his father was Japanese, and not American, Russian, Chinese, or English." The court added that the Fourteenth Amendment had been added to the U.S. Constitution to make sure that the states could not treat groups of people unequally on account of race or color.

The Supreme Court also spoke of the United Nations Charter and the fight against racism abroad during World War II. The court asked: How could the United States be faithful to the international pledge of the United Nations Charter of human rights and freedoms for all people without distinctions of race, if America had state laws which kept people from owning land on account of race? California's land law, said the court, was a sad reminder of the racist ideas of Nazi Germany. This decision by the Supreme Court encouraged Asian Americans to challenge the unfair land laws. Four years later, after several court cases, California reversed its land law. The California Supreme Court ruled that the state could not deny landownership to people who were not eligible to become U.S. citizens. This meant that Asian immigrants, who did not yet have citizenship rights, could at least own land in America. One of them expressed this new freedom in a haiku, a traditional Japanese poem:

> *Land laws faded out,*
> *It is comfortable now—*
> *This America.*

The court rulings showed that people's ideas were changing, especially in California. In 1956, the Japanese American Citizens League (JACL) launched a drive to remove

California's old land laws from the books, even though they had already been overturned by the state supreme court. The JACL used this drive as an educational campaign against racial prejudice. By this time, the United States had entered the civil rights era. The U.S. Supreme Court had outlawed racially segregated schools in the historic case of *Brown v. Board of Education,* and the Montgomery, Alabama, bus boycott had demonstrated that a growing number of people were demanding equal rights for African Americans. More people were beginning to share the idea of racial equality. This was proved in California when the people of the state voted two-to-one to remove the land laws from the state's books. The JACL hailed this as a triumph for the Japanese immigrants, "whose love for the land kept them steadfast through years of discrimination."

Meanwhile, the Japanese and other Asian immigrants had become eligible for citizenship. The McCarran-Walter Act, a law passed in 1952, allowed Asian immigrants to be naturalized—that is, to become citizens of the United States. Before 1952, only white immigrants could be naturalized. But the McCarran-Walter Act opened the door to citizenship for Asians, many of whom had been living in the United States for years. The passage of the act brought joy to Japanese Americans. "It was the culmination of our dreams," exclaimed Harry Takagi of the JACL. "The bill established our parents as the legal equal of other Americans; it gave the Japanese equality with all other immigrants, and that was a principle we had been struggling for from the very beginning."

Many elderly Japanese immigrants, who had been forced by the restrictive laws to be "strangers" in America, were eager to become citizens in their adopted country. By

1965, some 46,000 of them had taken their citizenship oaths. One was my aunt Mitsue Takaki. For her, citizenship was part of a decision she had made years earlier in Hawaii. In 1931, after learning that her husband was going to be sent back to Japan by the immigration authorities, she had decided to stay in Hawaii with her three children. Decades later, as a grandmother, she passed her citizenship test. Her children remember how proudly she stood before a federal judge and took the oath of allegiance as a citizen of the United States. Many of the Japanese immigrants who were naturalized after 1952 were in the twilight of their lives, yet they were happy to fulfill their long-held dream of citizenship. A newly naturalized citizen felt an urge to celebrate the moment in poetry:

> *Going steadily to study English,*
> *Even through the rain at night,*
> *I thus attain,*
> *Late in life,*
> *American citizenship.*

Like the Japanese immigrants and their children, Americans of Chinese descent found their role in American society changing in the years after World War II. China and the United States had been allies during the war, but good relations between the two countries did not last long after the war ended in 1945. China was plunged into civil war between communist and non-communist forces, and in 1949, the communists under the leadership of Mao Zedong won control of the country and established a communist state called the People's Republic of China. The former rulers of China fled to the island of Taiwan and set up a rival government there. The United States supported Taiwan and refused to recognize the People's Republic of China. Contact was broken off between the United States and the People's Republic.

These developments in China splintered Chinese communities in America. Chinese intellectuals who were sympathetic to communism, as well as workers' associations, cheered Mao's triumph. Other groups, such as the Chinese business associations in San Francisco and elsewhere, supported the campaign to overthrow communist rule in mainland China.

Americans of Asian descent made significant contributions to the war effort, both in the armed forces—as in the case of these Japanese American soldiers from the army's intelligence unit— and as civilian defense workers.

In 1950, the People's Republic of China became involved in the Korean War, which pitted U.S. forces against communist troops. This set off hysterical anti-Chinese reactions in the United States. Many white Americans, fearful of the spread of Asian communism, imagined a new peril in their own communities. A Chinese American woman recalled those days: "The Korean War affected us at the beginning in that

we were taken for Communists. People would look at you in the street and think, 'Well, you're one of the enemy.' "

"The whole atmosphere here then was fear," a Chinese American man explained. "If you weren't careful, you could be thrown into a concentration camp." In late 1950, Congress passed a law that said that communists could be rounded up and sent to camps during a national emergency. This law was an ominous and menacing reminder to the Chinese in America. During World War II, Japanese Americans on the West Coast had been sent to concentration camps. Now, during the Cold War, the same thing could happen to Chinese Americans. The Chinese were forced to prove their loyalty to the United States.

In 1955, after an American official in Hong Kong warned that spies from the People's Republic of China could use false citizenship papers to get American passports and enter the United States, U.S. authorities began investigating thousands of Chinese Americans, charging that their passports were based on false birth certificates. As the government charged Chinese residents with fraud and sent those who were found guilty out of the country, waves of fear swept through Chinese communities. People who had entered the United States with false papers—not because they were spies but in order to bypass a U.S. ban on Chinese immigration—were especially frightened.

To help in its investigations, the government created the "confession program." Chinese residents who had entered the United States illegally were encouraged to come forward and confess their guilt to the Immigration and Naturalization Service (INS). They were then required to give details about the status of all their relatives and friends, which meant that

Fifteen hundred Japanese Americans from California, uprooted by the war, created a new agricultural community for themselves in Bridgeton, New Jersey.

a single confession could involve dozens of people. In return for the confessions, the government allowed those who confessed to remain in the country as long as they were not involved in spying or other disloyal activities. Thousands of people participated in the program. In San Francisco alone, 10,000 Chinese confessed. Ninety-nine percent of all confessors were allowed to stay in the United States.

The federal confession program spread poisonous divisions and distrust within the Chinese community. "We knew the FBI was keeping a close eye on us, and we even suspected there was an informer among us," said a man who belonged to the Min Ching, an organization that supported Chinese communism. "I guess that's one thing all of us feel bad about now, that we had to be suspicious of each other." He explained that entire families had to be fearful: "Say, if a Min Ching member is discovered to have false papers, his whole family will be affected because probably they didn't have the proper papers either. So they'll go from you, to the uncle who brought you in, his wife, and it goes on and on."

Gradually, as the anti-communist hysteria died down during the 1960s, pressure on the Chinese residents of the United States was eased. By this time, the civil rights movement was gaining strength, and the history of all minorities in the United States was entering a new stage. Soon the immigration laws would change, enlarging Asian American communities with a new wave of immigrants.

A Chinese American family celebrates the Chinese New Year.

Chapter Two

The Second Wave Begins

WORLD WAR II CHANGED MORE THAN THE LAND AND citizenship laws. It also led to the reopening of the gates of Asian immigration. During the global military conflict, Americans had begun to see that the United States could not claim to be a democracy as long as its immigration laws were openly racist, keeping whole groups of people out simply because they were Asian. In the 1940s, the U.S. government opened the door to some Asian groups, but it also set strict limits. Asians could come again, but only a handful of them. In fact, only a token number of Asians were allowed to enter the country. Japanese and Korean immigrants were still prohibited. The Philippines and India could send only 100 each year; China's quota was only 105. The law was far more generous to European immigrants. For example, Poland had a yearly quota of 6,524.

Many Asians found ways around the restrictive quotas. After World War II, the navy continued to recruit sailors in the Philippines, and thousands of Filipinos entered the United States through this door. After the communist victory in China, 5,000 Chinese professionals and students found themselves stranded in the United States, and most of them were permitted to stay as immigrants.

The most important loophole, however, was the War Brides Act, which allowed Asian wives and children of U.S. servicemen to enter without being counted in the annual quotas. Thousands of Chinese American soldiers married women in China and brought them to the United States. Between 1946 and 1953, more than 7,000 Chinese women entered the country as war brides. "Right after the war," remembered Harold Lui of New York Chinatown, "guys came home from the army with wives from China." Filipinos, too, were bringing wives to the United States. After becoming citizens through service in the U.S. armed forces, Filipino men sent for their families. In the 1950s, the Korean War began a new Korean immigration: Between 1950 and 1965, 17,000 Koreans entered the United States, most of them as wives of American citizens.

America's immigration policy loosened a bit more in 1952. The McCarran-Walter Act, the same law that allowed Asian immigrants to become naturalized U.S. citizens, permitted increased immigration from what was called the "Asian-Pacific Triangle." This was a large geographic region that included India. Although it opened the door of immigration a little wider, this new law still discriminated against Asians. Countries within the "triangle" could send only 100 people to America each year. European nations could send many more.

While the United States was battling communism abroad in the Cold War of the 1950s and 1960s, it faced pressure for fairer immigration laws. To make good its claims of democracy, the United States felt compelled to drop the restrictive immigration quotas. In 1964, Secretary of State Dean Rusk urged the country to reform its immigration laws. He warned that the old, discriminatory system was hurting U.S. relations with other countries. The peoples of Africa, Asia, and Latin America heard the United States praise the virtues of democracy, but they noticed that Americans did not always practice what they preached.

At the same time, the Civil Rights movement had begun to awaken the moral conscience of America, condemning racism in all its forms—including immigration policies. Black Americans, along with progressive whites, launched massive protests against racial segregation and discrimination. After countless civil rights marches and demonstrations led by Martin Luther King, Jr., and others, the U.S. Congress outlawed racial discrimination in the Civil Rights Act of 1964.

The movement for equal rights within the United States focused on the treatment of blacks, but the concept of racial equality also had affected people who were seeking to enter the country, including Asian immigrants. If America's goal was equality for all its citizens, then immigrants seeking entry must also be treated equally. "Everywhere else in our

Japanese immigrants, many of them longtime residents in the United States, are sworn in as U.S. citizens in a San Francisco court in 1953, one year after the McCarran-Walter Act made them eligible for citizenship.

national life, we have eliminated discrimination based on national origins," said Robert Kennedy, the U.S. attorney general, to Congress in 1964. "Yet, this system is still the foundation of our immigration law."

Some Americans were against immigration reform. A patriotic organization called the Daughters of the American Revolution protested that the immigration laws should continue to favor immigrants "whose background and heritage most clearly resemble our own"—white European immigrants, in other words. But the momentum for change, driven by the civil rights movement, could not be halted. "Just as we sought to eliminate discrimination in our land through the Civil Rights Act," said one congressman, "today we seek . . . to eliminate discrimination in immigration to this nation composed of the descendants of immigrants."

In 1965, a year after the Civil Rights Act, Congress passed a new Immigration Act. Under this law, 20,000 immigrants each year would be allowed to enter the United States from each Asian country. As permanent residents or citizens, immigrants would be allowed to bring their spouses, children, and parents to the United States. Such family members would not be counted as part of the quota; thus thousands of additional immigrants would be allowed to enter the country.

The new law reflected a change in the way Americans thought of their country. No longer did everyone see the United States as a uniformly white society. The civil rights movement had offered a different vision of America, a vision of multiracial equality. The time had come to change the old ideas about who could become an American, and the 1965 Immigration Act would be a large part of that change. It would transform the United States once again into a golden door for

Ethnic Chinese refugees from Vietnam arrive in Los Angeles in 1979.
The second wave of Asian immigration included those escaping from war as
well as those seeking new opportunities.

immigrants from a "different shore," pushed from their home-lands in Asia by poverty or strife and pulled to America by their hopes and dreams.

The 1965 Immigration Act began a new chapter in the history of Asians in America. It opened the way for a second wave of Asian immigration. Before 1965, an overwhelming majority of America's immigrants came from Europe, but today, one out of every two immigrants comes from Asia. Mainly as a result of this second wave of immigration, Asian Americans have soared in numbers—from about 1 million, or less than 1% of the U.S. population, in 1965 to 5 million, or nearly 3% of the population, in 1985. In the 20 years from 1965 to 1985, four times as many Asian immigrants entered the United States as had entered during the previous century.

The second wave of immigration not only increased the Asian American population but also changed the balance of the various Asian groups. In 1960, more than half of all Asians in the United States were Japanese. A quarter of all Asians were Chinese, a fifth were Filipino, and Koreans and Asian Indians each accounted for only 1% of the total Asian American population. By 1985, the Japanese no longer made up the majority of Asian Americans. The largest groups were Chinese and Filipino—each made up 21% of the Asian American population. The rest of the population represented a greater variety than in earlier years: 15% Japanese, 12% Vietnamese, 11% Korean, 10% Asian Indian, 4% Laotian, 3% Cambodian, and 3% other.

The second-wave newcomers are strikingly different from the earlier immigrants. They include significant numbers

*Asian immigration after
1965 has been ethnically
diverse. Among the newcomers
have been many from Southeast
Asia, including this Vietnamese
woman and her child.*

of professionals and people from the cities, in contrast to the
farmers and rural folk of the past. The immigrants who came
after 1965 have been entering an economy that depends on
high technology such as computers and on service businesses
such as restaurants and banks, rather than on manufacturing
and agriculture. Unlike the Asian immigrants of the first wave,
they have not become railroad workers and farm laborers in

The tide of new immigrants since the mid-1960s has provided labor for ethnic industries, such as the garment business in New York's Chinatown.

America. They have been seeking jobs in an economy that demands increasingly complex skills.

In general, earlier immigrants who did not speak English could get work as laborers, because it was not necessary for them to communicate well. The recent immigrants, however, have faced language barriers, for many jobs today are closed to those who cannot speak, read, and write English. Another difference between the earlier and recent immigrants is that the first immigrants arrived as solitary workers. Most of them left their families behind in the homeland, planning to return after working in America and saving money. But the recent immigrants have been arriving as families rather than as single men. They have also been coming as settlers, planning to stay permanently in the United States. Many of them have cut their ties to the homeland. If they encounter hardship and setbacks in the United States—as many of the earlier immigrants did—these recent settlers have not been able to say that the situation in America is only temporary and count the days until they return home. They *are* home.

The second wave of Asian immigration has included far fewer Japanese than the first wave. Only about 4,000 Japanese immigrants arrive in the United States each year, far below the quota of 20,000. In the first half of the 1980s, Japanese immigrants accounted for less than 2% of the total immigration from Asia. One reason for the drop in Japanese immigration is that Japan experienced a huge burst of economic growth and prosperity in the decades following World War II.

With the decline in new arrivals from Japan, the Japanese American population in the United States consists

*A rally in New York celebrates the beginning of
diplomatic relations between the United States
and the People's Republic of China in 1979.
U.S. president Jimmy Carter is pictured on the
left, Chinese chairman Hua Guofeng on the right.
Many recent Chinese immigrants have fled from
the People's Republic and reached the United
States by roundabout routes.*

mostly of people born in America. Japanese Americans are largely English-speaking; very few third- and fourth-generation Japanese Americans know any Japanese. The Japantowns in American cities, the neighborhoods where early immigrants clustered and opened their shops and restaurants, have not been culturally renewed, for they lack the energizing presence of new immigrants. "Many second- and third-generation Japanese Americans have moved to the suburbs," said the head of a Japanese youth group in San Francisco. "And there are too few new immigrants from Japan to fill their places in Japantown."

But while Japanese have not been flocking to the United States, immigrants from other Asian countries have been entering America in greater numbers than ever before. How is this new immigration reshaping American society?

Chinese women immigrants who lack resources for child care are limited to jobs in garment factories and other places where they can take their young children with them to work.

Chapter Three

San Yi Man: New Immigrants from China

THE CHINESE WHO HAVE COME TO AMERICA SINCE 1965 are called the *San Yi Man* ("new immigrants"). They are the third largest group of immigrants in the United States, after Mexicans and Filipinos. Between 1965 and 1984, they numbered 419,000—almost as many as the 426,000 Chinese who came to the United States between 1849 and 1930. This huge second wave of Chinese immigration has helped change the ethnic shape of American society. In 1960, before the second wave began, the Chinese population in the United States numbered only 237,000, half the size of the Japanese population. Twenty years later, the Chinese population had jumped to 812,200, and there were more Chinese than Japanese people in the country.

The Chinese community itself had changed. Before 1965, many Chinese Americans were the American-born children of early immigrants. But the flood of newcomers after 1965 meant that by 1980, nearly two-thirds of all Chinese people in America had been born in Asia. Once again, Chinese America has become mainly an immigrant community.

More than half of the second-wave Chinese have settled in two states, California and New York. Their presence has been revitalizing Chinatowns there. New York City, the first choice of many new Chinese immigrants, has seen a population explosion in its Chinatown. Before the 1965 Immigration Act, New York's Chinatown never had more than 15,000 people; by 1985, it was home to 100,000.

The new immigration can be described as a chain migration of family members. One of the new immigrants explained: "My brother-in-law left his wife in Taiwan and came here as a student to get a Ph.D. in engineering. After he received his degree, he got a job in San Jose. Then he brought in a sister and his wife, who brought over one of her brothers and me. And my brother's wife then came."

This family history is typical. During the 1960s, Chinese students began flocking to U.S. colleges and universities. Because students were not considered immigrants, they could enter freely. By 1980, half of the 300,000 foreign students in America were from China and other Asian countries. After graduation, thousands of Chinese students were able to find jobs and became eligible to apply for immigrant status.

Once they had become immigrants, they could bring their wives and children to America. Then, a few years later, once they had become U.S. citizens, both the husband and wife could bring their parents. They could then sponsor their brothers and sisters, who, in turn, could arrange for the entry of their own spouses, children, in-laws, and so on. One person, originally coming to the United States as a foreign student, could thus begin a long chain of immigrants.

Unlike the first immigrants, who were mostly peasants from the Chinese countryside, the second-wave immigrants came mainly from the cities. They represented not only the working class but also the professional class. Between 1966 and 1975, nearly half of all Chinese immigrants were managers, professionals (including scientists, doctors, and engineers), and technical workers. Unlike the first-wave immigrants, they did not come to America planning to work for a few years and then return to the homeland. They were eager to become American citizens. Three-fourths of the Chinese people who entered the United States between 1969 and 1978 became naturalized citizens within eight years.

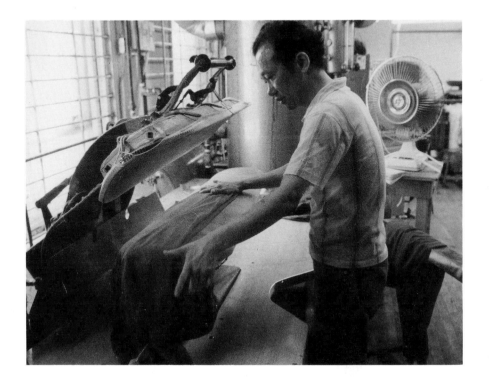

Gender is an important difference between the first and second waves of Chinese immigration. Most of the first immigrants were men, but the second wave has included more women than men. More than half of the Chinese who entered the United States between 1966 and 1975 were female.

Most of the second-wave immigrants first fled from the People's Republic of China, the communist country on the Chinese mainland. They usually entered the United States from a second point of departure, such as the British colony of Hong Kong or the island nation of Taiwan, rather than directly from mainland China. After the United States opened trade with the People's Republic in 1979, however, the com-

Lacking English language skills, some of the new arrivals from China have found themselves confined to low-paying jobs in the old urban Chinatowns.

munist country was allowed to have its own immigration quota.

The second-wave immigrants came to America for a variety of reasons. Like many of the first-wave immigrants who fled from the turmoil of civil war in 19th-century China, some of the recent newcomers sought refuge from political conflict and instability in China. Betty Chu is one of these. After the communists came to power in China in 1949, she accepted the idea of communism and became a high-school teacher. But during the 1960s, she saw how people were beginning to live in fear. People suspected of having anticommunist thoughts were harassed by young communists and sent to remote provinces. Worried about this rising political repression, Chu and her husband made a "secret" decision to leave China. Her husband got permission to visit his brother in Hong Kong and then stayed there; Chu followed with her son. Her husband's brother had gone to the United States as a student years earlier and had become an American citizen. He sponsored the Chu family as immigrants in 1969.

Another second-wave immigrant, Xiu Zhen, was also a high-school teacher in China, but she was accused of being a spy. "Maybe I wrote some letters and mentioned something political," she explained later, "but I was not political at all." Her hair was cut off and she was put in jail. "Everybody was placed in this one room," she said. "I was there about one year and two months with fourteen other people. We didn't sleep there. We went home at night, but they made us work very hard. . . . Sometimes the Red Guards burned me with cigarettes. They kept saying, 'We have to wash your brains.'" In 1974, Xiu was allowed to visit her mother in Hong Kong. "I said I had to go to her because she was sick. Of course that was not the real reason." From Hong Kong, she came to the United States.

Like the 19th-century pioneers who were drawn to America by dreams of making their fortunes, some second-wave Chinese immigrants were pulled to the United States by the hope of a brighter, more prosperous future. "The people told me that coming to America will be just great," said an immigrant who arrived in 1968. "There was hot running water, cold water and even warm air [heating]. The water in the village countryside was filthy and very unsanitary, filled with pigs' and other animals' waste. Any place with 'clean water' must be like 'the sky above the sky.' America is 'Heaven.'"

The immigrants of the second wave saw America as a place of possibilities. Wing Ng came to the United States in 1975 at the age of 23. "The reason why I wanted to come to the United States is that I heard it is really freedom," she said. "That's the first thing. And the second was education." Wing joined her father in Hong Kong, but she found that her opportunities for work and education there were extremely limited. "In Hong Kong it is difficult to go to college, too. Only two universities. Too many people. Too much competition for jobs. The people in Hong Kong don't like the others coming in and taking the jobs. So the only jobs you can get are in the factories."

America would be a land of greater opportunity, the *San Yi Man* believed. But when they arrived, they frequently found themselves in impoverished Chinatowns in cities like San Francisco and New York. Shrouded behind the tourist image of the Chinatowns as charming and colorful communities was the reality of the ghetto: poverty, unemployment, and crowded housing. The immigrants also faced economic discrimination. In 1960, Chinese male workers in New York City and San Francisco earned only about 56 to 68 cents for every dollar earned by white male workers. Chinese women fared even worse. They earned less than half as much as white women.

The unemployment rate for men in San Francisco's Chinatown was much higher than the city's average. Chinatown was also crowded, with 885 people per acre, compared with only 82 people per acre in the other sections of the city. In New York's Chinatown, more than a third of all families

Self-employment, in a shop, restaurant, or small sidewalk business, is common among recent immigrants. Many start their own businesses as a response to limited job opportunities in the larger society.

lived below the poverty level. More than half of the housing units in both Chinatowns were old and run-down. Both communities had extremely high rates of suicide and tuberculosis. Many inhabitants were elderly men, bachelors from the first wave of immigration, living out the remainder of their lives in tiny rooms in shabby hotels.

The different class backgrounds of the old and new immigrants led to a split in the Chinese American community, between working-class menial laborers and educated, middle-class professionals. New York City has the "Downtown Chinese," who are mostly waiters and seamstresses, and also the wealthier "Uptown Chinese." In southern California, there are Chinatowns in central Los Angeles and also in more prosperous suburbs like Monterey Park.

Monterey Park has been called "America's first suburban Chinatown." It is a striking contrast to the old urban Chinatowns. The Chinese have become the largest ethnic group in Monterey Park, totaling more than half of the 61,000 residents in 1988. During the early 1980s, the city elected its first Chinese mayor, Lilly Chen. But not everyone welcomed the new Chinese presence. In 1986, for example, a sign at a gas station near the city limits showed two slanted eyes and the words: "Will the last American to leave Monterey Park please bring the flag."

The Chinese residents of Monterey Park are not allowing such bigotry to discourage them. They are building an American city in their image, and they can afford to do so. Many of the city's Chinese residents are wealthy. Chinese real estate agents call Monterey Park a "Chinese Beverly Hills," and BMWs and other expensive cars are parked on the streets. The Chinese own two-thirds of the property and businesses

黄紹輝 Sui Fei Warren Wong

Six-year-old immigrant Sui Fei Wong becomes Warren Wong in a ceremony at a New York school. Some Chinese parents have given their children more American names, hoping the change will help the youngsters enter the mainstream of American society.

in the city. Monterey Park has Chinese markets, restaurants, and retail stores as well as Chinese theaters, churches, doctors, and lawyers. It is a complete Chinese community.

But most of the second-wave immigrants have gathered in the old urban Chinatowns. More than three-fourths of the people in the New York, San Francisco, and Los Angeles Chinatowns are foreign-born. Unlike the suburban Chinese professionals, they are mostly low-wage laborers. Most of them do not have even a high-school degree. They also lack English language skills. More than half of the

Chinese residents of New York Chinatown speak English poorly or not at all. "This does not mean that they are not trying to learn," explains a community organizer. "In fact, there are at least two dozen English-language schools in the community. . . . Thousands of working people squeeze time out from their busy schedules to attend classes. However, the real problem is that they do not have the opportunity to use English on the job or with other Chinese immigrants. They soon forget the scant English they have learned."

Poor English skills and limited job opportunities make for a vicious cycle. "Chinese people have lower incomes because first, the language problem," says a second-wave immigrant. "If you know just a little English, you can go to an office and get a job cleaning up. It has more security, more benefits. But how are you going to get a job like that if you don't know a little English? And how are you going to learn English if you have to work twelve hours a day, six days a week and then come home and take care of your family?"

Unable to speak English, many Chinese immigrant women have no choice but to work as seamstresses. A study of garment workers in San Francisco's Chinatown found that nearly three-quarters of them have husbands who work, but they have to work too, to help the family barely get by. Yet most of these women are still solely responsible for all household chores. With this double burden, they had to look for jobs in the garment industry, where they could have flexible work hours and could bring their babies to sleep near them in the factory.

While women work mostly in the garment industry, men are often employed in the restaurants. The director of an English language school in San Francisco's Chinatown ex-

An immigrant from Taiwan works toward his degree in engineering. Education has drawn thousands of young Chinese people to America. Many of them are then able to get jobs, become U.S.citizens, and bring their families here to join them.

Alleged members of a criminal gang in New York's Chinatown Like all segments of American society, the Asian American community has its share of crime and violence.

plains how recent immigrants are locked into low-paying restaurant jobs: "Most immigrants coming into Chinatown with a language barrier cannot go outside this confined area into the mainstream of American industry." One man who had recently arrived in the United States said, "Before I was a painter in Hong Kong, but I can't do it here. I got no license, no education. . . . I want a living, so it's dishwasher, janitor or cook."

Many of the recent immigrants who were professionals in their home countries have had to take menial jobs in America. "There are innumerable instances of former doctors, teachers, accountants, and engineers who took jobs as janitors and waiters when they first arrived," said one woman. "Some stay in the rut because of language problems or because they are afraid to venture out and compete vigorously in the job market." One couple held teaching jobs in China: the wife was a mathematics teacher and the husband was a professor of

Chinese at a university. In San Francisco, however, she works as an office clerk and he as a janitor in a hotel. Both of them want to get ahead. Each night they study English until two in the morning.

Wei-Chi Poon and her husband, Boon Pui Poon, also experienced the problem of underemployment. Before they came to America in 1968, she was a biology professor and he was an architect in the People's Republic of China. "We had a really hard time right after we got here," she reported. "My husband was a very good architect, but because he couldn't speak English he could work only as a draftsman. His pay was so low that he had to work at two jobs, from eight in the morning till eleven o'clock at night." She worked in a laundry factory, packing uniforms into bags to be sent to Vietnam and earning only the minimum wage of $1.85 an hour. "The bags were at least 100 pounds each. At the time, I was one of the younger workers, so I had more strength than some of the

Outside the Chinese Consulate in New York in 1989, the Chinese Alliance for Democracy protests the killing of pro-democracy demonstrators in Beijing.

others. I got scared, wondering, 'Will I be doing this for the rest of my life?'"

She knew she would be trapped unless she learned English—but, as she said, "We were so busy working and so tired we had no time and energy to study English." A program funded by the Comprehensive Employment Training Act let her take English classes while working as a library assistant in the Chinatown branch of the San Francisco Library. She enrolled in the city's junior college and went on to do graduate study in library science. Now Wei-Chi Poon is the head of the Asian American Studies Library of the University of California.

The children of the second-wave Chinese face special difficulties and challenges. They feel confined in Chinatown, aware of the boundaries that limit their lives and their parents' lives. English is their second language, spoken outside the home. They also feel a strong obligation to do well in school, especially to please their parents. They are often reminded by their parents that education is the key to advancement in America. "Yes, with a good education, my children can find a better job," explained a Chinese mother, who had a college degree from a university in China and worked in a factory in the United States. "I don't want them to be like the first generation of Chinese immigrants here. They have to work so hard in those slave labor jobs."

The second-wave Chinese immigrants differ from earlier immigrants in many ways, but they often encounter the same prejudice and rejection that made the first immigrants feel that they were "eating bitterness." One immigrant student in Los Angeles told of insults from her white fellow students: "American students always picked on us, frightened us, made fun of us and laughed at our English. They broke our lockers, threw food on us in the cafeteria, said dirty words to us, pushed us on campus. Many times they shouted at me, 'Get out of here, you chink, go back to your country.'"

Like the Chinese men who came to California in the 19th century to mine gold, build railroads, and labor in the fields and orchards, the new Chinese immigrants have found themselves treated as "strangers" in America. Yet they continue to cross the sea to America, hoping to fulfill their dreams of work, school, family life, and community. They are keeping the urban Chinatowns alive, creating a Chinese American presence in the suburbs and universities, and helping to shape a multicultural America.

*At the U.S. Embassy in Manila, Filipinos wait for the visas that will
let them enter the United States. Filipino Americans are one of the fastest
growing segments of the Asian American population.*

Chapter Four

The Largest Group: The Filipinos

AFTER THE 1965 IMMIGRATION LAW WENT INTO EFFECT Filipinos began entering the United States in large numbers. But compared with the second-wave Chinese immigrants, the recent Filipino immigrants have been "invisible." The Chinese newcomers have concentrated in Chinatowns in large cities and built new Chinese suburban communities, while the Filipinos have spread throughout the country. Another reason Filipinos seem less visible in American society is that most of them speak English; in addition, many are Catholic and have Spanish names, and so they are sometimes confused with Hispanics. Yet the second wave of Filipino immigration has been much larger than the recent Chinese immigration. Between 1965 and 1984, 665,000 Filipinos entered the United States—200,000 more than the Chinese. Today, Filipinos are the largest Asian group in the United States, followed by the Chinese.

More than three-fourths of the Filipinos in the United States are immigrants. Unlike the first-wave Filipino immigrants, the second-wave Filipinos have come from the city rather than the countryside, and they have come to the United States as settlers rather than temporary workers. A majority of them have become U.S. citizens. In contrast to the earlier immigrants, who were mostly men, the recent Filipino newcomers have been mostly women. The new immigrants include professionals such as engineers, scientists, accountants, teachers, lawyers, nurses, and doctors. Between 1966 and 1970, for example, 10% of the Filipino immigrants were laborers, and 65% were professional and technical workers.

Many middle-class, well-educated Filipinos left the Philippines because of the corrupt, repressive government of President Ferdinand Marcos, who ruled the Philippines from

1965 until 1986. During this time, professionals in the Philippines became critical of Marcos' corruption and alarmed by his violations of human rights. Amnesty International, a worldwide human rights organization, reported on the torture of political prisoners in the Philippines in 1976, prompting a Filipino stockbroker who had immigrated to the United States to remark, "I know such things to be true." A Filipino business executive told the *New York Times* that the 1983 assassination of Benigno Aquino, who led a movement against the Marcos government, was one of the major reasons he had moved to the United States with his family. At that time, the Philippines seemed to be sinking into oppression and terrorism.

But people also have emigrated from the Philippines for economic reasons. Many of those who left were highly educated but could not find skilled or professional jobs in the Philippines. Describing this "brain drain," the *Los Angeles Times* said in 1972, "There is an overabundance of a well-educated middle class in the Philippines, and a startling number of them cannot use their special learning after graduation. The Philippine government's own statistics indicate that only 60% of today's college graduates are employed in any more than menial jobs."

A very high percentage of people in the Philippines are college graduates. Many of them, however, have faced extremely limited job prospects. In 1970, a million people had college diplomas, but only about half of them could find suitable jobs. "We have more than two hundred registered civil engineers in the city," said the mayor of one Philippine city. "Where would I get them employed! So the problem is a surplus of professionals."

College-educated Filipinos have suffered not only from a scarcity of jobs but also from low wages. "Wages in Manila are barely enough to answer for my family's needs," said one immigrant. "I must go abroad to better my chances." A nurse compared wages in the two countries: "My one day's earning here in America is more than my one month's salary in Manila, especially when I do a plus eight [overtime]." Explaining why he and other professionals came to the United

Thirty-two years after the end of World War II, 52 Filipino men who had served with the U.S. armed forces in the Philippines were sworn in as U.S. citizens in San Francisco.

States, an accountant said, "It is common [in the Philippines] for middle-class Filipinos to work at two or even three jobs because of the high cost of living. I have paid as much as $7.50 per pound for chicken there because food is not in abundance as it is here. . . . In the United States, hard work is rewarded. In the Philippines, it is part of the struggle to survive."

Images of American abundance, carried home by the *Balikbayans,* the immigrants who return to the islands for visits, have drawn frustrated Filipinos to the United States. One man went back for a visit after working in the United States for 10 years and told his friends, "If you work, you'll get milk and honey in America." Other Balikbayans described the United States as a "paradise." The governor of one island province reported, "The Balikbayans say that in the United States people from the Philippines are given the opportunity to work for better pay, better medical conditions, better social security. . . . For example medical practitioners who migrate and become American citizens have very good opportunities in the United States, both personally and professionally."

Nurses and doctors have played a great part in the recent immigration. Filipino nurses and doctors seem to be everywhere in the medical services in the United States. During the 1970s, one-fifth of the 20,000 nurses who graduated from school in the Philippines came to the United States. The flow of Filipino doctors has been even greater. Forty percent of all Filipino doctors in the world practice in the United States, and the medical school of the University of Santo Tomas in the Philippines has been a major supplier of doctors to the United States. By 1974, there were 7,000 Filipino doctors in the United States. There were 1,000 in New York, where the total Filipino population was only

45,000. Filipino doctors have been on the staff of every hospital in New York and New Jersey.

But coming to America has not necessarily increased opportunities for Filipino medical professionals. In the United States, Filipino doctors must pass an examination administered by the Educational Council for Foreign Medical Graduates in order to qualify for private practice, internship, or hospital residence. This test and additional state requirements often force Filipino doctors to do further study and find temporary work as nurses' aides and laboratory assistants. "In Los Angeles, there are several hundred Filipino unlicensed physicians working in jobs that are totally unrelated to their knowledge and expertise," Dr. Jenny Batongmalaque told the California Advisory Committee to the U.S. Commission on Civil Rights. "They have no opportunity to review or to attend review classes. They cannot afford to pay the tuition and they have no time because they have to earn a living to feed themselves and their children." A Filipino attorney told the committee, "Filipino doctors are accepted as professionals as defined by the Immigration and Naturalization Service and the Department of Labor. However, when they come here, they are not allowed to practice that profession under which they were granted the visa because of the State's strict licensing procedures. That's an inconsistency." This inconsistency forced one Filipino surgeon to work in a restaurant as a meat cutter. He did not tell his bosses that he was a doctor, but later, in an interview, he smiled as he remarked, "They thought I was very good at separating the meat from the bone."

Pharmacists educated in the Philippines have met even greater difficulties. They are not even allowed to take the licensing examinations in many states. In California, for ex-

A doctor from the Philippines practicing in Los Angeles in 1976. Thousands of Filipino doctors and nurses entered the medical profession in the United States.

ample, only graduates of schools on the state Board of Pharmacy's approved list can take the test to receive their licenses, but that list has never included a foreign school. As a result, hundreds of Filipino pharmacists have been kept from practicing their profession.

Filipino veterinarians have also encountered obstacles. After arriving in America in 1973, a veterinarian explained that she had hoped to practice in her field. But she learned that she would first have to pass an English test, satisfy a one-year clinical internship at an accredited veterinary hospital without pay, and pass the California state licensing examination. To support her family and herself while she prepared for the examination, she had to work as a clerk in an insurance company. She finally obtained her license—after seven years. "Foreign educated or trained professionals are as good as the Americans," she said in an interview, adding that she believed the licensing requirements were set up to discourage foreigners who might compete with graduates of American schools for jobs.

Many Filipino immigrants have found themselves underemployed, working at jobs far below those for which they were trained. In Salinas, California, during the 1970s, more than half of the new immigrants who had been employed in professional and technical occupations in the Philippines worked as clerks, salespeople, and wage laborers. Meeting socially, they playfully called each another by their former titles, such as "Doctor," "Professor," or "Attorney." Reported the *New York Times*, "[Filipino] lawyers work as file clerks, teachers as secretaries, dentists as aides, engineers as mechanics."

Sometimes Filipino professionals are steered toward low-level jobs simply because they are Filipino. For example, a college-educated newcomer went to a government employment office to find a job and was advised to look for work as an agricultural laborer. The disappointed job-seeker said, "He simply asked me if I were a Filipino and without opening my folder he gave me an address of a vegetable grower."

Old-timers and recent immigrants alike, Filipinos have faced a struggle to be accepted in the United States. They

have confronted racial prejudice, job discrimination, and un-deremployment, yet their presence in America is large and growing. They continue to seek the dream of freedom that America offers. Like the earlier wave of immigrants from the Philippines, they have come, to use the words of writer Carlos Bulosan, "searching for a door into America" in order to build new lives. "Would it be possible," Bulosan asked, "for an immigrant like me to become part of the American dream?"

By the 1990s, Filipino Americans numbered more than a million. More than one-fifth of all Asian Americans are of Filipino descent.

65

*A Korean shopkeeper in Brooklyn, New York, whose greengrocery
was picketed by blacks. Koreans have frequently suffered discrimination
when they succeed in neighborhoods where opportunities are not available
to other minorities.*

Chapter Five

From Professionals to Shopkeepers: The Koreans

AFTER THE PASSAGE OF THE 1965 IMMIGRATION ACT, the Korean population in the United States began growing, both in the total number of Korean Americans and also in how Koreans compared with other Asian American groups. In 1960, only 1% of all Asian Americans were Korean. By 1985, 11% were Korean.

This second wave of immigration made Koreans much more visible in America. For decades, the Korean population in Hawaii and on the U.S. mainland had been around 10,000. Between 1965 and 1985, it jumped to half a million. By the beginning of the 1990s, more than 100,000 Koreans were living in New York, where a cluster of Korean restaurants and stores had appeared on Broadway between 23rd and 31st streets. Los Angeles County was the home of 200,000 Koreans. A new community had sprung up along Olympic Boulevard in Los Angeles. "It's called Koreatown," *Newsweek* magazine reported in 1975. "What used to be Mexican-American, Japanese and Jewish stores and businesses are now mostly Korean, with giant Oriental letters spread across their low-slung storefronts." This concentration of Korean-owned grocery stores, churches, gas stations, travel agencies, barber shops, insurance companies, restaurants, and nightclubs caused one Korean immigrant to say, "One does not feel that one lives in America when one lives on Olympic Boulevard."

Most of the recent Korean immigrants have been from the college-educated middle class rather than from the farming and working classes. Surveys of Koreans in New York and Los Angeles have found that about 70% of them had college degrees when they arrived in the United States. Many had been professional and technical workers in Korea. Unlike the first-wave immigrants who left Korea as temporary laborers, planning to return, these new immigrants have come to America as permanent settlers, bringing their families with them. A majority of them have applied for citizenship. "The fascination of America for the Korean immigrants," said one immigrant in 1975, "is to come to a free and abundant country, and breathe in its air of freedom, and make plans for a new life such that they are changing their destinies, which were fatalistically determined by tradition and history in the old country."

Immigration reform in the United States made it possible for large numbers of Koreans to enter the United States at a time of rapid economic and social change in Korea. In the 1960s and 1970s, South Korea developed modern industries to produce goods, including clothing and electronic equipment, to be sold in other countries. To keep the prices of Korean goods low enough that other countries would buy them, industries paid their workers low wages. The government helped keep down wages by outlawing labor strikes. The Korean government also held down the price of rice, which meant that many farmers could not make enough money from the land. The farmers then had to come to the cities to look for factory jobs. Millions of Koreans streamed from the countryside into the cities, which became overcrowded. At the same time, South Korea was having a population explosion, making the overcrowding even worse. "Korea's population density is one of the world's highest," explained an official of a Korean bank in California in 1976, "so the natural tendency is to seek some better opportunity than at home where competition is too keen." For many Koreans, that "better opportunity" seemed to be the United States.

Seoul and other Korean cities simply did not have enough jobs—especially for educated professional and technical workers. Thousands of professionals began leaving Korea and going to Germany, Brazil, Argentina, Canada, and the United States. "I could not find a job after obtaining my B.S. in chemical engineering at Chungnam University," said one man. He applied for an overseas labor contract and worked in Germany as a miner for three years. "I was afraid that I would become unemployed again if I returned to the home country," he said. "I wandered through some European nations for a while, but I could not find a proper place to settle. Upon arriving in the United States, I found a lot of jobs waiting for me."

Many medical professionals have left Korea for the United States. Between 1965 and 1977, more than 13,000 Korean physicians, nurses, pharmacists, and dentists entered

Teaching Korean in Los Angeles. A large number of recent immigrants from Korea are highly trained professionals such as teachers, engineers, and doctors.

69

the United States. South Korea's modern new medical training schools have produced more graduates than the country could employ; in 1973, for example, nearly three-fifths of the nurses who graduated in Korea could not find jobs. "The schools in Korea produce many qualified doctors," said a Korean immigrant who sponsored the immigration of his brother and sister, both doctors. "The truth is they have more doctors in Korea than they can support—not more than they need, but American cities can use more too." Unable to find jobs in the major cities and unwilling to practice in rural areas, many Korean doctors left Korea for the United States.

Arriving in the United States, Korean nurses and physicians have been drawn to the East Coast, where there has been a shortage of medical workers. In 1980, one-fourth to one-fifth of all Korean immigrant nurses and doctors were working in New York City. "Korean doctors of New York," a Korean American sociologist observed, "are the most 'successful' of Korean immigrants. They represent the largest group of Korean suburban houseowners; most of the Korean residents of Scarsdale are immigrant doctors. With MD plates on their cars, the Korean doctors in New York can display their highly esteemed status in white suburban neighborhoods."

But the appearance of high status conceals some frustrating realities. Korean doctors have often found themselves confined to inner-city hospitals and shunned by white doctors. They tend to find jobs in fields such as anesthesiology and radiology instead of high-status fields such as surgery and internal medicine. Beginning in the late 1970s, Korean doctors also saw a drop in the demand for physicians and a new wave of discrimination against foreign doctors when they applied for positions in hospitals.

Many Korean doctors have not even been able to practice medicine in the United States. They discovered they simply could not support a family and also prepare for the many tests they had to take, including an English language test and an examination in their special medical field. As a result, some Korean doctors, especially those with limited English language skills, have been working as hospital orderlies and nurses' assistants.

Korean pharmacists, too, have had trouble practicing their professions in the United States. In California, Korean pharmacists cannot even take the state licensing test because Korean pharmacy schools are not on the list of approved schools. Seung Sook Myung's story is typical. She had been a pharmacist in Korea for 10 years before coming to Los Angeles in 1974. Because she was not able to take the state licensing examination, she could not work as a pharmacist in her new home. She became a knitting machine operator at a plant where nine out of ten workers were Korean. Like many other educated, professional Korean immigrants, Myung found herself locked into low-wage work.

Kong Mook Lee, another pharmacist who immigrated to Los Angeles, invested his money in a garment factory when he found that he could not practice pharmacy. "The only thing my wife knows is sewing," he said. "The only thing I know is pharmacy. Pharmacy is impossible; so sewing is the only way." Lee counted at least 300 experienced Korean pharmacists in southern California alone who had to change occupations. "We never expected to lose our profession at the same time as we immigrated to this beautiful and wonderful country," he said. "Today, most of us find ourselves in a job which is inconsistent with our qualification and experience. We are suffering from starvation wages."

Korean teachers and business administrators have also found limited job prospects in America. In fact, many Korean professionals in the United States are underemployed and must work at jobs below their level of training and education. A survey in Los Angeles in 1978 found that only about one-third of immigrants with professional training were able to find jobs in their fields. Korean immigrants who were office workers in their home country have become auto mechanics, welders, radio and television repairpersons, gas-station attendants, gardeners, and janitors in America.

For many Koreans, the answer to job discrimination and downgrading has been self-employment. They have

Koreans at an Asian American festival on Long Island, New York. The globe in the background was constructed for the 1964 World's Fair.

opened their own small businesses, such as wig shops, restaurants, liquor stores, and especially greengroceries (stores that sell fruit and vegetables). A writer for the *New York Times* observed that greengroceries had long been run by immigrants: "In fruits and vegetables, traditionally an immigrant business, first it was Jews . . . then Italians. And now up in the Bronx, it's the Koreans."

By 1983, Koreans dominated the produce business, owning three-quarters of the greengroceries in New York City. Korean greengrocers had become so numerous that they were competing with one another. "Across the street from me," remarked the new owner of a store in the South Bronx, "there is another Korean greengrocer; he bought his place from a Chinese four years ago. One block down, there's another Korean; he got his store from an old Jewish man who moved to Florida. Across from him, there's still another Korean. . . . Four Korean greengrocers in this crowded ghetto area!"

Because they have a very high rate of self-employment, the Korean newcomers are sometimes praised for their ethnic enterprise. How and why did so many of them become shopkeepers? Some of these immigrants obtained the money to open their businesses from small Korean cooperative credit associations. But they have also gotten loans from the Small Business Administration. Most important, however, many brought money with them, unlike the first wave of Korean immigrants. Beginning in 1981, Koreans have been allowed by the South Korean government to take up to $100,000 out of the country. Many immigrants bring with them the money to start a business in America.

In addition, the Korean newcomers have become shopkeepers at a crucial time in the history of American cities. Middle-class whites have been fleeing to the suburbs, abandoning the inner cities to blacks and Latinos. Older white merchants have been closing their businesses to retreat from the growing ghetto or to retire. "Before the Korean immigrants landed in this city, who were the greengrocers?" said Eugene Kang of New York's Korean Produce Association. "Most likely, they were Jewish and Italian, along with Greeks. The Jews and Italians and Greeks, they are third generation now. They want to go to law school. They are no longer taking care of father's business, which was greengrocer." These changes in the cities have opened opportunities in the economy for Koreans. To many immigrants, however, it seems strange and ironic that they left professional jobs in modern, industrialized South Korea to become old-fashioned shopkeepers in America. Streets lined with their shops and businesses have formed the cores of Koreatown in a number of cities, most notably Los Angeles, which has the largest Korean community anywhere outside Korea.

Many Korean immigrants have felt pushed into self-employment. "What else can I do?" asked a greengrocer who has master's degrees in city planning and mechanical engineering. "I need money but there are not good jobs for Koreans." A majority of Korean small businesspeople are college graduates; nearly four-fifths of the Korean greengrocers in New York have college degrees. Unable to find professional jobs, they would rather work for themselves than work as low-paid laborers.

The language barrier is another reason Koreans have turned to shopkeeping. Many of them have limited English language skills, which means that professional jobs are beyond their reach. "The language barrier," observed Ha Tai Kim, "virtually makes the newcomers deaf and dumb." Working long hours to make ends meet, most Koreans do not have time for English classes. But they can get by in greengroceries and other small businesses with only a limited knowledge of English.

Racial discrimination has also driven Koreans into shopkeeping. "When it comes to getting employment in American firms, factories, public and private institutions," charged Ha Tai Kim, "there is a great deal of difficulty in securing jobs due to discrimination and language barriers." Explaining why he resigned from a New York insurance company and became a greengrocer, a man who has a master of business administration degree from an American university said, "When I began to work for the insurance company, I met an Asian co-worker. This man had been with the company for several years. He was born in the U.S. His

A Korean-owned fish market. Korean American entrepreneurs have opened markets and greengroceries in many urban areas, filling an economic niche that was left vacant when earlier waves of immigrants migrated to the suburbs.

English was perfect. He was a hard worker. But he received only token promotions and was regularly bypassed by the white American workers who joined the firm after he did. I thought, 'This guy is good. But if he's not making it, neither will I.' So I left. In the store, at least, I'm in control of my own future."

Many Korean shopkeepers rely entirely on their families to operate their businesses. Korean immigrant women generally speak little or no English. Their job prospects in the general labor market have been very limited. But they are a source of unpaid labor for their husbands who own small shops. In a Korean-owned family business, everyone works.

The workday for Korean shopkeepers and their families begins early in the morning. A newspaper article described a typical day in the life of a Korean greengrocer in New York City: "Mr. Kim bought his store two years ago from a Jewish American for a total payment of $15,000—$10,000 for the store price and $5,000 in key money. He and his son daily purchase vegetables: at four o'clock every morning when the dawn is coming, they get up and drive to Hunts Point in the Bronx, where a city-run wholesale market is located. . . . In the market they run and run in order to buy at low prices as many as one hundred and seventy different kinds of vegetables and fruits. All the transactions are made in cash. At 7 o'clock they return to the store and mobilize the rest of the family members in order to wash and trim vegetables."

Out on the streets early in the morning darkness and in their stores until late at night, Korean greengrocers sometimes become targets for muggers and armed bandits. Many have been murdered. The physical labor of the business is punishing, too. "No matter how much energy, health, and stamina one may have," one greengrocer said, "one cannot stand more than two years of this daily toil." They complain of backaches and blood in their urine. "Sometimes you get so tired," another greengrocer sighed, "you cannot see the dollar in your hand."

A few greengrocers make handsome profits, clearing more than $100,000 a year. But most of them, for all their hard work and long hours, do not earn very much. The average income from an entire family's labor averages $17,000 to $35,000 a year.

But they work hard, many Korean immigrants say, for their children: "The first generation must be sacrificed." The parents must struggle so that the children can attend college and become professionals as their parents had been in Korea. The parents' lives may have become bleak in the United States, but they will do anything to brighten the futures of their children. In a poem describing the despair he felt for himself and the hope he nurtured for his child, a school janitor who had been a teacher in Korea wrote:

> I do not see, although I have eyes.
> Then, have I become blind? No, I have not.
> I do not hear, although I have ears.
> Then, have I become deaf? No, I have not.
> I do not speak, although I have a mouth.
> Then, have I lost my speech? No, I have not.
> I have become an old stranger who wants to raise a young tree
>   in this wealthy land.

Another former teacher in the old country, now a greengrocer, explained the purpose of his work and life: "The day before yesterday I kept my store closed all day long. That

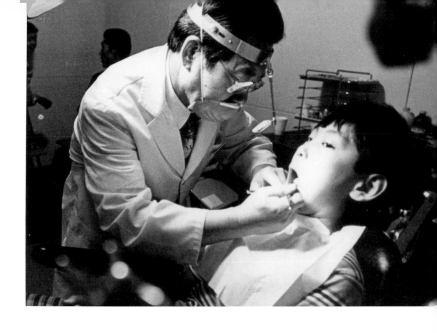

was my first day off since I started this business in 1976. My son, Jong Moon, graduated from Princeton University on that day. All my family members came. I am an old man, 65 years. I don't have a driver's license to get to the Hunts Point market. I can't run this business alone. But I have another son to help through college, Jong Won. I think I can last until both my sons go all the way up, to the highest educational degree."

A Korean lawyer in Los Angeles described the risks and benefits of Korean ethnic enterprise this way: "The immigrants come with a lot of money—$100,000 and $200,000. They sell their homes, everything they own in Korea and bring their cash with them. Many then open liquor stores in the black community. All their transactions are in cash. They are tough. They take risks and know they could get shot by robbers. . . . The Korean businessmen are like the Jews of the 1930s. They are hardworking and aggressive, but because of color they never reach the place where the Jews have reached."

To make their businesses profitable, some Korean business owners hire and exploit other Korean immigrants. They make their employees work long hours, and they pay them low wages, without vacations and health benefits. Korean employers find it easy to hire Korean workers who are desperate for jobs, because these workers are cut off from the mainstream economy by the language barrier and racial discrimination. The plight of these Korean laborers is often overlooked in the newspaper articles and news broadcasts that celebrate the success of Korean shopkeepers. Yet not all Korean immigrants share in that success. For example, one immigrant woman said that she worked in a garment factory and her husband worked 11 hours a day in a New York fruit and vegetable store owned by another Korean. "We came for a better life," she said wearily, "but we have not found it better yet. It is work, work, work."

Tension and conflict have sometimes arisen between Koreans and members of other ethnic minorities. In New York, Los Angeles, and other places where Korean businesses have sprung up in inner-city neighborhoods, people in the black and Latino communities sometimes resented the Koreans' success. They complained that Korean shopowners did not hire black employees; they also felt that many Koreans treated them disrespectfully. For their part, some Koreans viewed African Americans in terms of unfair stereotypes: blacks were seen as potential robbers or shoplifters. Each group often misunderstood the other's customs and attitudes. In many stores, resentment flared on both sides of the counter because neither person knew what the other was really thinking or feeling. The lack of communication was made worse by the language barrier, which kept many Koreans from talking freely with their customers.

In the spring of 1992, relations between Koreans and blacks in Los Angeles took a tragic turn when an explosion of rage changed the face of the city and forced Americans of all races to ask painful questions about social justice. The violent turmoil began on April 29, when a California jury declared its verdict in the trial of four white police officers charged with beating Rodney King, a black man, in the course of arresting him. The jury declared them not guilty, even though the beating had been captured on videotape and seen around the world. When word of the verdict reached the public, the streets of South Central Los Angeles exploded. An angry crowd attacked passing motorists and sacked nearby buildings. Despite pleas for order from city officials and community leaders, the violence swept into other areas. Crowds of mostly blacks and Latinos looted stores and set buildings on fire. The toll in hospital emergency rooms rose, and plumes of smoke thickened over the city. The mayor and governor declared a state of emergency and called in National Guard troops to try to restore order.

By May 1, the unrest had begun to settle down. The devastation was stunning: at least 58 deaths; nearly 2,400 injuries; 7,000 fires; more than 12,000 arrests; $800 million in damages; and 3,100 businesses damaged by fire, vandalism, or looting. More than 2,000 of these businesses belonged to Koreans. Many buildings in Koreatown and South Central Los Angeles were left in smoldering ruin. Many of the Koreans felt that they had been specially targeted by black gangs, who incited much of the violence. "It has been twenty years since Koreans came here," an immigrant woman said sadly. "Everything we worked for is now in flames. It burned in one day." Another said, "We Koreans worked hard to realize our dreams. Now nothing is left but ashes." As they picked through the rubble of their dreams, the dazed Koreans felt both anger and bewilderment.

A Korean American lawyer felt both "sad and angry" when she witnessed the turmoil in her home city of Los Angeles. "I hear generalizations on both sides of the black-Korean equation all the time," she said. "It troubles me a lot because black people are not all one way and Korean American people are not all another way. It is very dangerous to make generalizations about people." She added, "What is happening right now is not Korean history, it is American history."

Many Korean Americans agreed that the explosion in Los Angeles should not be regarded as a conflict between African Americans and Korean Americans. They felt that the rage that had been turned against them was an expression of the anger and frustration created by black unemployment, poverty, and despair. Yet in the aftermath of the destruction, many Korean Americans in Los Angeles suffered from depression. They felt that their "American dream" had been destroyed. They had always believed that if they worked hard, obeyed the law, and minded their own business, they would succeed. Now their work had gone up in smoke, and they could not understand why.

After the explosion, many Koreans felt despair. Yet some also expressed a determination to start over, to repair or restore what had been damaged. As the violence subsided and people began to assess their losses, a Korean community leader and member of the Black-Korean Alliance said, "People felt so powerless over the last few days. It was a tremendously traumatic experience. It will take some time to heal, and then we have to start the rebuilding process."

A South Asian newspaper vendor in New York City. Immigration from India and Pakistan brought new life to the South Asian American community in the 1970s.

ASIAN INDIANS HAD BECOME A DISAPPEARING MINORITY in the United States before World War II. By 1946, there were only 1,500 Asian Indians in the country. Although new immigrants were admitted after 1946, only a few were allowed to enter each year. The total population of Asian Indians remained very small. In 1960, only 1% of all people of Asian descent in the United States were of Indian descent.

Since 1965, however, immigrants from South Asia have been coming to North America in greater numbers than ever before. "South Asian" is a term used to include people from all parts of the huge Indian subcontinent. In addition to India, the subcontinent includes Pakistan, which was part of India until 1947, and Bangladesh, which was created as an independent nation from the eastern part of Pakistan in 1971. Although the majority of the recent South Asian immigrants to North America are from India, there have been some Pakistanis and Bangladeshis as well. There have also been a few immigrants from Nepal, a country on India's northern border, and Sri Lanka, an island nation off India's south coast that was formerly called Ceylon.

This second wave of immigration has brought new life to the Asian Indian community in America. After the 1965 immigration act, when people from India were able to enter the United States in greater numbers, this shrinking ethnic community entered a period of explosive growth and increasing variety. By 1970, 20,000 newcomers had arrived from Pakistan alone. Half of the Pakistani immigrants were from the region that had sent many immigrants to the United States early in the 20th century, in the first wave of Asian immigration. But unlike the first-wave immigrants, who were farmers, many of the second-wave Pakistani newcomers were highly educated professionals from the major cities.

The number of Asian Indians in the United States has climbed steeply, from 10,000 in 1965 to 800,000 in 1990. By 1985, Asian Indians represented 10% of all Asians in the United States. They are no longer a tiny minority isolated in the farming valleys of California, as was true for the first half of the 20th century. They have become very visible, especially in the northeastern states. More than one-third of all Asian Indians in the United States live in the Northeast; 18% of them live in New York alone. A section of Indian restaurants and stores on New York City's Sixth Street has come to be known as "Little India."

These new immigrants from India are very different from those of the first wave. The first-wave immigrants were almost all men, but the second wave of immigration has been equally divided between men and women. Unlike the first-wave immigrants, the recent newcomers have come to America not as temporary workers but as settlers, with every intention of staying. Many of them have shown their determination to become part of America by applying for U.S. citizenship. By 1980, more than half of them had become naturalized citizens.

Many of the first-wave immigrants had little or no education and spoke English poorly, if at all. But, in general, the second-wave immigrants speak English and are educated. In the decade after 1965, the immigrants came mostly from the professional class, which included doctors, teachers, and engineers. Said one of these newcomers, "The first Indian immigrants and the post-1965 Indian immigrants are two separate worlds. It is a class thing. They came from the farming, the lower class. We came from the educated middle class. We spoke English. We went to college. We were already assimilated in India, before we came here."

Indians from the professional class have continued to arrive in North America, but in the late 1970s and early 1980s the stream of immigration widened somewhat as the relatives of the earlier professional immigrants began to arrive. Some of these newcomers were less prosperous and well-educated than their fellow immigrants in the professions. Instead of entering law, medicine, or teaching, many of them turned to business. Beginning around 1980, the United States saw the arrival of many Asian Indians who became self-employed and opened their own small businesses. Some of these businesses, such as Indian restaurants and clothing shops, serve the needs of the growing ethnic community.

The immigrants of the early 20th century and those of recent years have had one important thing in common: their reason for coming to America. Like those who crossed the Pacific in the first wave of immigration, the second-wave immigrants have come mainly for economic reasons. By the 1960s, professionals in India found that their job prospects were severely limited. The number of people educated for the professions far exceeded the number of jobs available for them. Hundreds of thousands of Indians with college degrees were unable to find jobs. Unemployment was particularly serious for engineers and physicians. In 1970, for example, there were 20,000 unemployed doctors in India; four years later, the country had a "surplus" of 100,000 engineers.

Most of the second-wave Asian Indians have found that economic opportunities in North America are much better than those in their home country. Unlike some other newcomers from Asia, Asian Indians have not found themselves crowded into service jobs, such as restaurant work. In the late 1980s, Asian Indians had a lower percentage of people working in service jobs than any other Asian American group. They also had the highest percentage employed as managers and professionals; nearly half of all working Asian Indian Americans fell into this category, with 25,000 Asian Indian physicians and dentists, 40,000 engineers, 20,000 scientists, and 2,000 professionals in fields such as law and banking.

Yet many Asian Indian professionals have changed their occupations after arriving in North America. Rather than working in their fields of training, some college-educated immigrants can be found driving taxis and operating travel agencies, clothing shops, and luncheonettes featuring pizza, Greek dishes, or Indian "fast food" such as curry. Some operate newsstands in the subways of New York City. Newsstand owner Bawnesh Kapoor explains the advantages of his job: "You don't need a lot of capital to start. You don't have inventory problems because you normally turn over your entire inventory in a week. You don't have accounts receivable problems. You don't have to worry about changes in fashion." Asian Indians have also been investing in the motel business. More than one-quarter of the hotels and motels in the United States are owned by Asian Indians.

While many of these people have become self-employed by choice, others have found themselves pushed into self-employment by discrimination. Asian Indian technicians and engineers, for example, complain about how they hit what has been called the "glass ceiling"—a point where they can see the higher-paying management jobs but cannot get into them. "The only jobs we could get were based on merit," explained Kumar Patel, head of the material science division of AT&T. "That is why you find most [Asian Indian] professionals in technical rather than administrative or managerial positions." Similarly, an Asian Indian engineer who had worked for Kaiser for some 20 years told a friend, "They [management] never even give you [Asian Indians] an executive position in the company. You can only go up so high and no more." Frustrated by limited opportunities to advance in their careers, many Asian Indian professionals have turned to opening their own businesses.

In communities across the land, Asian Indian Americans are making their presence felt. In Philadelphia, where 25,000 of them had settled by the late 1980s, scores of restaurants, print shops, car dealerships, and clothing and jewelry shops owned by Asian Indians contribute to the city's economy. Asian Indian businesspeople in the community range all the way from a millionaire dealer in used luxury cars to an immigrant from a farming family who works for sixteen hours each day at his food stand in the city's university district. The Asian Indian community in Rochester, New York, numbers more than 500 families and includes a high number of doctors, university professors, and scientists. New York City, where the Asian Indian population skyrocketed from 6,000 in 1970 to more than 94,000 in 1990, has one of the largest Hindu temples in North America.

Asian Indian Americans have been trying to define who they are in their adopted society. In 1975, the issue of Asian Indian identity was raised by the U.S. government's Census Bureau, which examined the question of whether Asian Indians belonged to a "minority group." A government official decided that they did not, stating that persons of Asian

An immigrant from Pakistan, his wife, who is from Sweden, and their children enter the United States as new citizens. Between 1965 and 1970, 20,000 immigrants came to America from Pakistan, a country that was formerly part of northwestern India.

Indian descent "are regarded as white." Some Asian Indians agreed with this view. Among them were the leaders of the Chicago-based India League of America. The India League argued that it would be a mistake for their group to claim minority group status. According to the League, Asian Indians in America were not truly disadvantaged, and other Americans might turn against them if they appeared to benefit from programs, such as Equal Employment Opportunity, that were intended to help the victims of discrimination.

But many other Asian Indians believed that Asian Indians should be considered a minority group. The Association of Indians in America pointed out that Asian Indians, like African Americans and other Asian groups, were discriminated against because of their skin color. In a statement to the U.S. Civil Rights Commission in 1975, the Association declared: "The language of the Civil Rights Act clearly intends to protect those individuals who might be disadvantaged on the basis of appearance. It is undeniable that Indians are different in appearance; they are equally dark-skinned as other non-white individuals and are, therefore, subject to the same prejudices." The Association concluded that Asian Indians were "disadvantaged for reasons of racial discrimination."

In 1976, leaders of the Association took part in a government-sponsored meeting to discuss the ethnic categories that would be used in the 1980 national census. The meeting included representatives from the Pacific Islander, Chinese, Japanese, Filipino, and Korean communities as well as the Asian Indians. They decided that Asian Indians should be recognized as a distinct group, and the Census Bureau agreed to change the category to which immigrants from India and their descendants belonged. Instead of being included in the "white/Caucasian" group, they would be counted as "Asian Indian."

Asian Indians are proud of their ethnic heritage, yet they also want to be identified as Americans. Hamida Chopra explained it this way. She came to the United States after 1965 to join her student husband, thinking her stay in America would be only temporary. But 23 years later, she said, "America is my home." Although she chose not to become a U.S. citizen, she thinks of herself as "an American." But she is also

Indian. She speaks only Urdu in her home and has taught her daughter the language and culture of the ancestral land. She always wears Indian clothing, which on formal occasions means the distinctive sari—a long piece of cloth worn so that one end forms a floor-length skirt and the other is draped over the shoulder. When she first arrived, people looked at her as a "foreigner," Chopra recalled. "But now these days," she noted, smiling, "they look at me and have no curiosity. American society is open, able to absorb differences in cultures and dress. I feel that the definition of what is 'American' has become broader."

The definition of an "American" *is* becoming broader and more multicultural. At the same time, however, a few people, feeling threatened by the growing diversity that they see around them in streets, stores, and schools, have lashed out in hate crimes against people whose ethnic backgrounds are different from theirs. In recent years, Asian Indians have been among the victims of violence fueled by prejudice.

Violence broke out in 1987 in Jersey City, a town in northern New Jersey where about 15,000 Asian Indians were living. In a series of incidents, people of Asian Indian descent were harassed by teenagers, many of whom were Puerto Ricans. Some of the Asian Indians suffered only verbal abuse, shouts of "Hindu! Hindu!" and other taunts and insults. Other victims were slapped or pelted with eggs, stones, and empty soda cans. Attackers threw stones at the houses of some Asian Indian families, and Asian Indian places of worship were vandalized. Tragically, the violence did not stop there. A man of mixed Indian and Iranian descent was beaten so severely that he died; another man, an Asian Indian immigrant, was beaten into unconsciousness on a city street.

In the wake of these events, a local newspaper printed an anonymous letter that was said to be from a racist group called the "Dotbusters"—a reference to the small dot called the *bindi* that some Asian Indian women wear on their foreheads for religious reasons. The "Dotbusters" said, "We will go to any extreme to get Indians to move out of Jersey City," and threatened more violence against people of Asian Indian descent. The writer of the letter claimed that the "Dotbusters" targeted their victims by looking for Asian Indian names in the phone book.

The Asian Indian community reacted with fear and outrage, calling for increased investigation of racial crimes and for better police protection. Five hundred Asian Indians marched through Jersey City to urge police action with the slogan "We want justice!" Young men formed community watch groups to patrol their streets and neighborhoods. Concern spread far outside Jersey City. Asian Indians around the United States discussed the troubling issue of anti-Indian prejudice and racial crime, both in local meetings and in the pages of *India West* and *India Abroad*, newspapers that serve Asian Indians in America. Asian Indians knew that the problem was not confined to New Jersey; they had suffered harassment and vandalism in Chicago, Long Island, New York City, and elsewhere. In December 1987, a few months after the beatings in Jersey City, Asian Indian community leaders from all over the country attended a national meeting and formed an organization to combat anti-Indian racism and racial violence through public demonstrations, the courts, and political action.

Much of the violence against Asian Indians has been economic in origin. In Jersey City, where some of the attackers were members of the large Puerto Rican immigrant community, the outbreak showed the resentment of one group of immigrants against another that seemed to be outdoing them in jobs and income. Many of the area's factories and large industries have closed, and unemployment is high, especially among unskilled and semi-skilled laborers. Asian Indians have opened shops, restaurants, and other businesses in and around Jersey City, but because of their traditions of shared family enterprise, they usually employ their relatives, which has contributed to the frustration of non-Indians who cannot find jobs. Puerto Rican immigrants, some of whom lack English-language skills, are especially hard hit by the shortage of jobs; if they cannot speak English, they are passed over for service jobs that require them to deal with the public.

In addition, racial antagonisms reflect the ways different groups view one another through negative stereotypes. In the late 1980s, some young members of the Asian Indian community realized the need for multicultural education to combat this ignorance. After the outbreak of ethnic violence in Jersey City, Asian Indian students at New York City's Columbia University formed a group called Indian Youth Against Racism (IYAR). They were concerned about the anti-Indian hostility in New Jersey and elsewhere, but, as one of the founders said, "We also wanted to . . . align ourselves with other groups which also suffer from racism—blacks, Hispanics, and even some of the groups which were minorities a few decades ago."

Members of IYAR have worked to reduce racism in several ways. Some of their actions have been political; for example, they lobbied for the passage of a New Jersey law that set new, harsher penalties for crimes that had an element of racism. Other activities have been educational in nature. IYAR members helped write a pamphlet for teachers that outlined some key aspects of Indian culture, hoping to bring to non-Indians a greater understanding of customs that are shaped by Indian tradition and religion.

IYAR members felt that the best way to destroy racial myths and stereotypes was to educate young people. In discussions that followed the Jersey City incidents, IYAR came up with the idea of confronting racism in the schools. "They were convinced that racism should be fought from the earliest stage, and while it might not be easy to change the racial attitude of the adults, it was worth trying to do so with young students," explained an educator who worked with IYAR to develop a teaching project for a Jersey City high school. The project brought together several dozen students of different races for two weeks, during which racial stereotypes were brought into the open and replaced with facts and shared experiences.

Similar educational projects are now being used to counteract racial tension in many school systems. They are promoting communication among ethnic groups. As a young American-born Asian Indian woman said, "We are here with whites, blacks, Jews, Hispanics, and we have to learn to live together and respect each other's hopes, desires, and ambitions."

A refugee mother and child at a holding camp in Hong Kong, after fleeing Vietnam by boat in 1987.

Chapter Seven

Fleeing from Southeast Asia: The Refugees

IN 1964, THERE WERE ONLY ABOUT 600 VIETNAMESE people living in the United States. They were students, language teachers, and diplomats from South Vietnam, a country in Southeast Asia that had begun to receive increasing attention in the news.

Vietnam had been part of a French colony called Indochina since the late 19th century. Then, beginning during World War II, the Vietnamese Communist party under the leadership of Ho Chi Minh fought the French to regain their country's independence. This war ended in 1954. The French and the Vietnamese communists agreed to divide Vietnam temporarily into two parts, North and South Vietnam. The communists believed that a nationwide election would soon establish a new government that would reunite the two parts. Instead, however, a new government was formed in South Vietnam, with the support of the United States, to counter the communist government in North Vietnam, which was backed by China and the Soviet Union (now Russia). The split of Vietnam became permanent. The election was never held, and civil war erupted.

In the early 1960s, President John F. Kennedy sent U.S. forces to Vietnam. This was the start of U.S. involvement in the Vietnam War. The war ended in 1975, when the United States withdrew and South Vietnam was taken over by North Vietnamese forces. Thousands of people from South Vietnam fled to the United States to escape the communist takeover.

These immigrants were different from the other Asian groups already in America. Unlike the Chinese, Japanese, Koreans, Filipinos, and Indians, the Vietnamese refugees did not choose to come to America. They were driven out of their homeland by the powerful events surrounding them. Most of them were in the military or connected with the fallen South Vietnamese government and were fleeing from the North Vietnamese troops. A week before the collapse of the South Vietnamese government in April 1975, 10,000 to 15,000 people were evacuated from South Vietnam. Then, in the frenzied last days of April, 86,000 Vietnamese were airlifted out of the besieged country.

Panic gripped the people. "On those last days of April," remembered a refugee, "[there was] a lot of gunfire and bombing around the capital. People were running on chaotic streets. We got scared. . . . We went to an American building where a lot of Americans and their Vietnamese associates were ready to be picked by American helicopters." The city shuddered under relentless missile bombardments; homes and buildings were burning everywhere.

> *Fires spring up like dragon's teeth*
> *At the standpoints of the universe:*
> *A furious, acrid wind sweeps them toward us from all sides. . .*
> *All around, the horizon burns with the color of death.*

Frightened people rushed to get out of Saigon, the South Vietnamese capital. From the roof of the American embassy, hundreds climbed frantically onto helicopters. Others drove to the airport, where they abandoned their cars with notes on the windshields: "For those who are left behind." Terrifying images were seared into the refugees' memories. One woman never forgot the sight of people trying desperately to get aboard a plane. "I saw people jamming the door and women and children could not get on," she said. "The shelling came closer and then the plane took off with people still hanging at the door."

Others left by boat. A young Vietnamese girl recalled how she and her family scrambled to board a small boat with 50 other people. "I could hear the noisy firing guns, screams from injured people on the beach, and cries of little children," she wrote later. "While standing on the boat, I couldn't think of anything. It was not until sunset, when it was dark, that I stopped staring back and started worrying about the waves. It rained all night. I was all wet and cold. Holding each other, my brother and I prayed. The next day at noon time, we reached an American ship. As soon as the ship lowered one of its stairs, everybody climbed up the stairs without any order.

Desperate refugees scramble for passage on a U.S. helicopter as Saigon falls to the North Vietnamese forces in April 1975.

Men, women, and children were pushed aside and dropped into the sea. Some were crushed between boats. I carried my youngest brother and went up that stairs with fear." During the next few weeks, 40,000 to 60,000 Vietnamese escaped in boats to the open sea. They were picked up by American navy ships.

The refugees had no time to prepare for departure. Some did not even know for certain who would be going and who would be staying. Said one refugee, "Mother came along to the airport. Then at the last minute she stayed behind because the number of children staying was larger than those leaving." Others thought they would be gone for only a month or two: "My mother would never have left her other six children behind if she thought she wasn't coming back."

Some 130,000 Vietnamese refugees found sanctuary in the United States in 1975. They generally came from the educated classes. Many of the heads of these households had completed high school and attended college. Almost two-thirds of them could speak English. Most came from the urban areas, especially Saigon; they were more Westernized than the general population of Vietnam. After arriving in the United States, the 1975 refugees were placed in processing camps, usually on military bases. From the camps they were spread throughout the country, but they soon began to gather in communities such as Orange County, California. They were the first wave of Vietnamese refugees in America.

Meanwhile, in Vietnam, the fighting had stopped. The new communist government had reunified Vietnam and now began reorganizing society. People who had been associated with the old government were sent to camps to be "re-educated" in communist philosophy. Private property was seized by the state. Large numbers of city-dwellers were forcibly moved into the countryside. Thousands of Vietnamese, particularly urban business and professional people, were ordered to "go to the country to do labor, the hard jobs, to make the irrigation canals, sometimes for one month, sometimes for two, or three months." One of these displaced workers said, "Life was very hard for everybody. All had changed! . . . I could see no future for me in Vietnam, no better life! I wanted to escape."

More than 600 men, women, and children fled from Vietnam to Malaysia aboard this vessel.

Thousands did escape—21,000 in 1977, 106,500 in 1978, more than 150,000 in 1979, and thousands more later. They took their wives and children and boarded crowded, leaky boats, risking their lives at sea where storms threatened to drown them and pirates waited to rob them and rape the women. Two-thirds of the refugee boats were attacked by pirates; many boats were attacked more than once.

> *Can you imagine human hair*
> *Flowing all over the sea,*
> *Children's bodies ready to dissolve*
> *As human meat dinners of fish?*
> *But they keep on leaving*
> *As humanity turn their heads away*
> *And still they serenely*
> *Throw themselves into death.*

Thirteen-year-old Thai Dang remembered how she left Vietnam in 1981. "I just wanted to embrace my dear friend, Trang, tightly, telling her that I would be leaving Saigon in an hour, that she would always remain my friend," she said. But she had to keep her planned escape a secret. "So, I left briefly, as if chased by a ghost, before they could see my eyes getting red. . . . I was yearning to capture each familiar scene, each beloved face of the place I had lived and grown up." But as Dang and other refugees were on their way to the boat, they were "discovered and hunted like beasts" by the Vietnamese forces. "I ran, fell, and ran for my life in the unknown darkness of a strange forest, totally oblivious to my bleeding wounds." Her mother placed her on a small boat and waved goodbye, and Dang wondered, "Who was to guarantee that I would survive in the dark sea?" At sea, the refugees were attacked by Thai pirates. Said Dang, "The pirates, wearing almost nothing but frightening tattoos, jumped into our boat with axes and guns to rob and beat us. The air was saturated with the most disheartening cries. . . . We were literally begging on our knees."

Luong Bot Chau told a similar story. She and her husband, along with several dozen refugees, sailed away on a small vessel. Off the coast of Thailand, their boat was attacked by Thai pirates. The pirates chopped off one of her husband's fingers to get his ring and then tried to slit his throat. "But the knife they had was too blunt," she said later. Instead they clubbed him to death and threw his body into the sea. Then they dragged the young girls up to the deck and systematically raped them. "We heard them scream and scream," Luong Bot Chau cried. "We could not get out, because the pirates had nailed down the hatch." Many of the refugee girls and women were raped during their desperate attempt to escape from Vietnam.

The survivors floated to Thailand, where they had to live in squalid refugee camps for months, often for years. From the camps, they went to countries like Australia, Canada, and France. This second wave of refugees was more diverse than the 1975 group. It included educated professionals as well as fishermen, farmers, and storekeepers from the countryside and small villages. Most of them did not speak English. Many of them were ethnically Chinese, members of Chinese communities that had existed in Vietnam for centuries. When China invaded Vietnam in 1979, these ethnic Chinese fled Vietnam to escape discrimination.

By 1985, there were 643,200 refugees from Vietnam in the United States. "Remember these are the people who

Braving pirates and storms, Vietnamese refugees in tiny boats survived the dangerous voyage to Hong Kong.

were on our side," an American veteran of the Vietnam War said. "They have a right to come to this country as refugees. They just need a home." But often they have felt unwelcome in America. Like earlier Asian immigrants, the Vietnamese have experienced the stings of racial insults. They have been viewed as a threat in areas where there are shortages of housing and jobs.

At first, many of the Vietnamese refugees saw their exile from their homeland as temporary. They hoped to return to Vietnam someday. A 1977 survey showed that 41% planned to return to Vietnam to live. As the years passed, however, many of the refugees gave up this dream and began to regard the United States as their new home. "If Vietnam were a free country," said Loan Vo Le, who had fled from Saigon in April 1975, "I would like to go back. I miss my family so much. But we couldn't stay. I'm afraid we are too spoiled by life here, the conveniences, the opportunities, the education and the freedom. . . . I feel like a Vietnamese American, but inside I'm still Vietnamese."

The refugees tried to recreate their traditional culture in the new Vietnamese American communities. But many realized that the old ways could not be strictly maintained in the United States, especially in terms of men's and women's roles. "In Vietnam, the women usually were dependent on the husband a great deal," a refugee explained. "Then when we came here, the Vietnamese women had jobs. This made the men feel extremely insecure." Some of the women have found new opportunities in America. Winnie Che, for example, began working as a waitress in 1981. "My first job I felt so happy," she said. "I can work! Somebody will hire me here." In 1983, Che opened her own restaurant in Carnation, Washington. "In Vietnam, I would be just a housewife: clean up, cook dinner. Here, if you work hard, you can do what you want."

Thrust abruptly into a very different culture, the Vietnamese have found their traditional family ties severely strained. "Back in Vietnam the family is something precious for us—father, mother, children," explained Tran Xuan Quang. "But in coming here, we saw that the family here is too loose. The father works in one place, the mother works in another and they don't see each other at all. Sometimes the father works in the morning and the mother works in the afternoon and the children go to school. When they get home, they hardly see each other at all."

Sometimes parents are saddened by the new behavior of their children. Many young Vietnamese Americans have begun to lose their Vietnamese language. "I hated it when Americans teased me about my language," complained Mai Khanh Tran. "Maybe that's why I don't talk in Vietnamese in front of an American anymore. When I first came here, I used to talk in Vietnamese but ever since they teased me I

Nguyen Cao Ky, once the premier of South Vietnam, made a new life as the operator of a shrimp-processing plant in Louisiana. Not all Vietnamese refugees had the resources to go into business in their adopted countries; many found the adjustment to American life economically as well as emotionally difficult.

don't feel comfortable doing it anymore. At home I do because my parents always talk Vietnamese and I'm trying to preserve what I have for as long as possible. But I can feel it's slipping away."

Thousands of Vietnamese young people have entered college as high achievers, but others found themselves on the streets. Many of them came to America alone, sent by their parents, who hoped that the children would obtain an education and become American citizens. Without families, though, many of these children had difficulty surviving. They lived in motels and hung out in cafés and pool halls. Some joined gangs.

Most refugees knew they would face adjustment problems in America, yet they wanted to become part of American society. They hoped to be accepted as Vietnamese as well as Americans. "We cannot look at the future without knowing who we are. We must remember our roots, our heritage," insisted one Vietnamese American. In addition to cultural challenges, the refugees faced economic difficulties. Some were wealthy and arrived in the United States with enough money to open their own businesses, but most needed to find jobs. Yet many of them could not get jobs with the same income and status they enjoyed in Vietnam. "In Vietnam I was a history and geography teacher," a refugee said. "Here I worked on many different jobs—brick layer, carpenter, clerk typist, salesman, truck driver, delivery man. I felt frustrated and depressed because I had social status and possessions in Vietnam. Here I didn't have anything." The Vietnamese have also experienced problems of racial discrimination. Some feel that racism has kept them from being hired or promoted.

"I am a patient man," a Vietnamese refugee said. "If I have to start over again, I believe I will make it someday. I believe I will become self-sufficient as an auto mechanic. Most refugees have only one hope: to have a job and become a tax payer." Many Vietnamese have achieved much more. In California, where they have concentrated, they have created their own Vietnamese communities, sometimes called "Little Saigons." Vietnamese own many businesses in Orange and Los Angeles counties.

The signs of Vietnamese American settlement have become a permanent part of the American landscape. Most cities boast Vietnamese restaurants or even whole neighborhoods; many classrooms include Vietnamese students. The flow of arrivals from Vietnam has increased since 1982, when an agreement between the U.S. and Vietnamese governments opened the way for 20,000 Vietnamese each year to join family members who were already in the United States. In 1990, the Vietnamese population in America consisted of 614,500 people who have brought their dreams and determination to enrich new communities in America.

Another group of refugees from Southeast Asia is less visible and less well-known than the Vietnamese. These are the Laotians, refugees from Laos, a neighbor of Vietnam. In the 1960s, the Vietnam War exploded into Laos. After 1975, when the communists came to power in both Vietnam and Laos, Laotians who had supported the United States scrambled in panic for safety, seeking sanctuary as refugees. Members of three Laotian ethnic groups fled to America: 150,000 ethnic Lao and 90,000 Mien and Hmong.

"This is a good life here," said a Lao refugee. "No war. No death. No hunger." But many Laotians find American

culture almost impossible to understand. "It is easier to move the mountains than get used to American culture," observed a Lao. Another said, "We have been living in a jungle for a long time in Laos. This is another kind of jungle—a technological and bureaucratic jungle." This clash between two cultures has been especially sharp and painful for the Mien and Hmong, most of whom lived in remote, mountainous parts of Laos. Because they worked with the U.S. forces

Two of the 4,000 or so Vietnamese refugees who settled in the Michoud district of New Orleans.

against the communists, the Mien and Hmong felt an urgent pressure to flee Laos after 1975.

The refugees trekked to the Mekong River, crossing it on bamboo rafts and inner tubes to Thailand. From the crowded camps in Thailand they were sent to the United States. The Mien have settled in Seattle, Portland, Sacramento, Oakland, San Jose, and Long Beach. More than half of the Hmong have gathered in California, especially in Fresno, but Hmong are also located in places like Seattle, Providence, and Minneapolis–St. Paul. Life in America has involved dramatic adjustments for the Mien and Hmong. Coming from cultures that did not practice writing, they found it hard to understand how signs and letters could carry meaning. Accustomed to small communities where everyone knew everyone else, they found big cities confusing. They felt intensely lost in America, where they had to figure out how to use toilets and gas stoves and how to fill out welfare forms. Tasks such as figuring out how to pay a telephone bill were ordeals.

The Mien and Hmong have found that Americans generally do not know who they are or why they are in the United States. They have often been mistaken for Chinese and insultingly called "Chinks." In Eau Claire, Wisconsin, Hmong names stand out in the telephone directory, and the Hmong receive hostile phone calls. Angry voices tell them, "Go back to your country." Reflecting on the rejection the Hmong have experienced, Chou Lee of the Hmong Community Center in Eau Claire said, "Racism is like a wall. You cannot break through it."

Adjustment has not been easy. "When you pull a plant out of the ground without any soil around its roots—soil from where it was grown—and transplant it, the plant will have trouble surviving," explained Dang Moua, who became a hog farmer in California. "The Hmong never really thought about coming to America, never really believed they would have to leave Asia. Then suddenly we were here. . . . The technology and the Latin language of European or Mexican immigrants are much closer to America's. They have some dirt on their roots."

Many Hmong have been trying to plant their roots in new dirt by farming in Minnesota and California. But their traditional methods of farming do not work well in America. Explained one Hmong farmer, "We don't understand how to irrigate fields. In Laos, farmers just wait for rain. We don't understand marketing—one year farmers get high price for snow peas, next year almost nothing. . . . We thought to ourselves, if we farm, maybe we can be independent people again. But unfortunately, when we arrive in Central Valley [of California] we learn that you must have something else: lots of money."

Employment has been a desperate problem for the Mien and Hmong. Some try to make ends meet by selling handicrafts like needlework, silver bracelets, and earrings or by doing housecleaning and yard work. Most do not have jobs. Their rate of unemployment reaches as high as 90%. The Hmong may be in danger of becoming a permanent welfare class. A 1987 California study showed that many of the long-term welfare families were Hmong. Sadly, most Hmong are barely surviving.

Some have not survived. Seemingly healthy Hmong men have died suddenly and mysteriously. Doctors unable to explain their deaths refer to the "Hmong sudden death syndrome." Doctors have ruled out nerve gas, which was used in Laos, for only men have been affected. By 1988, more than 100 Hmong men had died. Said one community leader, "They had been soldiers for 15–20 years. They don't know how to start life over again. They don't know how to farm or to work in a factory." They also felt deep grief, despair, and confusion.

Depression is widespread among the survivors. In their struggle to live, to overcome their nightmares, the Hmong express their sorrow in song:

> Oh heaven, we Hmong did not want to flee from
> our country to a new country
> So far that we can no longer see our land
> We hear the birds singing, they fly in the sky
> They make us feel so lonely
> The sun is shining brightly

Many American families sponsored refugees, helping them make the transition to life in the United States. Here a host family in St. Louis teaches Vietnamese guests to play dominoes.

Are you as lonely as I am, or not?

I still have relatives back in my native country

I miss them more than most people can miss anyone.

My life in this country is sunny; it makes me feel like asking,

"Should I continue to live or is it better to die?"

I have no parents or relatives, only myself alone

Do you know how lonely I am?

The Hmong and Mien worry about whether they will be able to preserve their culture in their new home. "In America we don't wear our traditional clothing, not even grandmother," said one of them. "We only wear our traditional clothing on special days, and I will make my children only one set of clothes. When they grow up I don't know if they will marry American or Mien, so I will make only one set. Maybe when they grow up, they may forget our language."

Younger Hmong are gradually making an adjustment. They have learned to speak and write English, and many do not remember the old country. "Laos is like a dream," said Mao Yang, a college student in Wisconsin who escaped from Laos in 1976 at the age of eight. Her goal is to graduate with a degree in restaurant management and to own a restaurant in California someday. California appeals to young Hmong living in places like Wisconsin. "There are more Asians there," said Chou Vue, a student at the University of Wisconsin. "People don't look at you. Also I feel much more taller in California." Hmong college student Nou Xiong said that she felt like an "outsider" in Wisconsin and "more blended" in California. These young people see themselves as Hmong Americans and plan to make the United States their permanent home.

But the older Hmong and Mien spend much of their time in sadness. "Our village in Laos was ideal," an old Hmong grandfather recalled. "The mountains for rice fields were endless. There were big forests with game to hunt. Good streams. Bamboo. We never had to move far like other villages. Not until the Communists came." A Mien refugee said, "What I miss the most from Laos is my cow. I raised cows in the mountains. . . . Sometimes they would come from the jungle, and I would ride on the back of one cow." The Hmong and Mien are deeply and spiritually attached to the land they were forced to leave. "In Laos we believed there were spirits in the mountains," a refugee in San Diego explained. "Here, maybe the American Indians believe in spirits, but those"— pointing in the direction of the nearby Laguna range—"are *their* mountains, not ours."

The flood of refugees from Southeast Asia included a third major group, the Cambodians. Like the refugees from Laos, thousands of Cambodians were violently uprooted and chased from their homeland by death.

Located south of Laos and between Thailand and South Vietnam, Cambodia was also dragged into the Vietnam War. In 1970, the United States extended the war into Cambodia by sending bombers to destroy North Vietnamese supply lines and camps inside Cambodia. Five years later, while Saigon was falling to the North Vietnamese, a communist movement called the Khmer Rouge came to power in Cambodia, which was called Kampuchea during the Khmer Rouge regime. Under its leader, Pol Pot, the Khmer Rouge launched a brutal program to move Cambodia's urban population to the countryside and to destroy all Cambodians who were suspected of having American sympathies. "Pol Pot killed all the educated and professional people—doctors, lawyers, teachers," said Vacchira Loth, a refugee who escaped to Rochester, Minnesota. "If they knew I had been a medical school student, I would have been killed right away." Under Khmer Rouge rule, some 2 million people, about a third of Cambodia's population, died. Some were executed in mass graves called "killing fields"; others perished from starvation and disease. Fifteen-year-old Channa Cheng described the killing fields in a poem for her ninth-grade class in Seattle:

> *The people are hungry. The sun is shining.*
> *The women are working in the rice field.*
> *The babies are crying for their mother's milk.*
> *The guards are standing with arms around guns.*

To escape certain death, hundreds of thousands of Cambodians fled to Thailand in the 1970s and early 1980s. From disease-infested and crowded camps, more than 100,000 of them were resettled in the United States. Some of these refugees were educated people from the cities, but most were country folk, farmers from the rural areas. Many were women who had lost their husbands in the Cambodian conflict and had come here with their children. All of them carry the horrible psychological scars of the war and mass exterminations. "The tragedy during the war hurts inside when I remember what happened in the past," a tenth-grade boy told an interviewer. "I try not to think about it, but at night I dream and see my brother who they killed. I dream about him trying to find us. I dream they keep shooting him and shooting him until I wake up."

Many Cambodian refugees suffer from what psychiatrists call "post-traumatic stress disorder"—a depression that

A decade after arriving in the United States penniless and unable to speak English, Christopher Thang Thao became the country's first Hmong attorney.

had also afflicted the survivors of the World War II Nazi concentration camps. A 35-year-old Cambodian woman living in Oregon found she could not overcome the horror she had witnessed and experienced. After her husband was executed and her 18-month-old daughter had starved to death, she escaped to Thailand with her remaining children. She had left the killing fields behind, but the killing fields did not leave her. In Oregon each night "she would fall asleep, and in her dreams people came to kill her. During the day she was jumpy and easily startled, and when night came again she told herself to stay on guard and not fall asleep. Depressed, she was losing weight and had frequent thoughts of killing herself and her two children." With memories of the extermination still fresh in their minds, still haunting them, many Cambodians have experienced recurring nightmares, emotional numbness, loss of appetite, and withdrawal.

Cambodians would like to return to their homeland someday, but they realize the possibility is remote. Well into the 1990s, the Khmer Rouge continues to be a powerful and dangerous force in Cambodia, although it no longer rules the country. Many of the refugees who fled the Khmer Rouge have decided to make America their new home. "We want a chance to become part of this country," said one. "It is a chance for a new life. But, inside, the memories are still there. We won't ever forget."

The younger Cambodian refugees focus on the future rather than the past, but they often find themselves trapped between the two. Sathaya Tor, for example, had slaved for four years in a Khmer Rouge child labor camp. In 1979, the 12-year-old boy crossed minefields to escape to Thailand; he came to the United States two years later. In 1988, he enrolled at Stanford University, where he was the only Cambodian student. "Nowadays, sometimes I feel like a frog jumping from one world to the other: school, my family, being American, being [Cambodian]," Sathaya reflected. "In a way to be assimilated in another culture, you have to give up your own culture. With one foot in each culture, the wider you have to spread your legs, the more you could lose your balance. I'm at a point in my life where for the first time I feel vulnerable, and it's scary."

Another Cambodian refugee, Chanthou Sam, can understand Sathaya's feelings. She arrived in the United States in 1975 at the age of 12. Six years later, in recognition of her scholastic achievement and friendly personality, she was elected by her fellow students to be the Rose Festival Princess in Portland, Oregon. She spoke of her ambition to become an accountant, but admitted that this dream was at odds with her traditional culture. "A Cambodian woman is supposed to sit at home, cook, and clean house. I want to be somebody. I want my own job, house, and car before I marry. I want to be independent. It is very hard to be caught in the clash of cultures."

The Southeast Asian Americans are a diverse part of the Asian American population. They have come from different countries, cultures, and classes. They include tribespeople from the mountains as well as college-educated professionals from the cities, welfare families as well as wealthy business-men, and high-achieving university students as well as members of youth gangs. But despite their differences, the Southeast Asians share something unique. They came to America as refugees, not immigrants. Their experience has been different than that of the Asians who came to America before them.

Fleeing the horrors of war, they departed in panic, not knowing the country of their destination. They experienced the trauma of refugee camps and the terrible feeling of wondering whether they would have a place to begin life again. They worried about how they would be received when they reached their destination. Would they be welcomed or rejected? More than the earlier groups of Asian immigrants, the Southeast Asian refugees were truly uprooted. Lamented one of them, "They have no place they can call their own. They feel no sense of belonging to this land." In Texas, another refugee wrote:

In the obscurity of the night, a refugee cries
His tear of woe flooded on his eyes
He sobs for homeless life, the uncertainty of tomorrow. . . .

Still, these refugees from Southeast Asia, as well as the other Asian immigrants who have come to America since 1965, have been making their homes in the new land. They have struggled to learn Western ways while still striving to hold onto the heritages of their homelands. They have started businesses, and they have sent their children to schools and universities. They have created new ethnic communities and contributed new economic life to cities such as Chicago, Los Angeles, Oakland, Seattle, and San Jose. Together, these recent Asian Americans have been helping to redefine America, to make its society more multicultural. Crossing the Pacific, they share the vision of an earlier immigrant from Japan, who wrote:

All the dreams of youth
Shipped in emigration boats
To reach this far shore.

Chronology

mid-19th century	The first immigrants from China arrive in Hawaii and the U.S. mainland.
1880s	Japanese immigration to Hawaii and the U.S. mainland begins.
1900s	Immigration from the Philippines and India begins.
1924	The U.S. Congress passes the Immigration Act of 1924, which ends immigration from Asia.
1941	The United States enters World War II against Japan, Germany, and their allies.
1946	The United States allows a token number of immigrants to enter each year from China, India, and the Philippines.
1948	In the *Oyama* case, the U.S. Supreme Court rules that the law that prevents Asian immigrants from owning land in California is unconstitutional.
1952	The U.S. Congress passes the McCarran-Walter Act, which allows a slight increase in Asian immigration and also permits Asian immigrants to apply for U.S. citizenship.
1954	The U.S. Supreme Court outlaws racial segregation in public schools.
1964	The U.S. Congress passes the Civil Rights Act, an important step toward racial equality.

1965	The U.S. Congress passes the Immigration Act of 1965, which opens the door to a large second wave of immigration from Asia.
1975	The first wave of Vietnamese refugees arrives in the United States.
1979	The exodus of Cambodian refugees begins.
1979–82	The second wave of Vietnamese refugees reaches America.
1980–82	Hmong and Mien refugees arrive in the United States.

Further Reading

Chan, Sucheng. *Asian Americans: An Interpretive History.* Boston: Twayne, 1991.

Chen, Jack. *The Chinese of America: From the Beginnings to the Present.* New York: Harper & Row, 1981.

Choy, Bong-Yuon. *Koreans in America.* Chicago: Nelson-Hall, 1977.

Chuong, Chung Hoang and Le Van. *The Amerasians from Vietnam: A Country Study.* Folsom, CA: Southeast Asian Community Resource Center, 1994.

Cordova, Fred. *Filipinos—Forgotten Asian Americans: A Pictorial Essay.* Dubuque, IA: Kendall Hunt, 1983.

Daley, William. *The Chinese Americans.* New York: Chelsea House, 1987.

Freeman, James. *Hearts of Sorrow: Vietnamese American Lives.* Stanford: Stanford University Press, 1989.

Jensen, Joan M. *Passage from India: Asian Indian Immigrants in North America.* New Haven, CT: Yale University Press, 1988.

Kitano, Harry. *The Japanese Americans.* New York: Chelsea House, 1988.

Lehrer, Brian. *The Korean Americans.* New York: Chelsea House, 1988.

Mayberry, Jodine. *Filipinos.* New York: Franklin Watts, 1990.

Perrin, Linda. *Coming to America: Immigrants from the Far East.* New York: Delacorte, 1980.

Reimers, David. *Still the Golden Door: The Third World Comes to America.* New York: Columbia University Press, 1985.

Takaki, Ronald. *A Different Mirror: A History of Multicultural America.* Boston: Little, Brown, 1993.

Tenhula, John. *Voices from Southeast Asia: The Refugee Experience in the United States.* New York: Holmes & Meier, 1991.

Index

RONALD TAKAKI, the son of immigrant plantation laborers from Japan, graduated from the College of Wooster, Ohio, and earned his Ph.D. in history from the University of California at Berkeley, where he has served both as the chairperson and the graduate adviser of the Ethnic Studies program. Professor Takaki has lectured widely on issues relating to ethnic studies and multiculturalism in the United States, Japan, and the former Soviet Union and has won several important awards for his teaching efforts. He is the author of six books, including the highly acclaimed *Strangers from a Different Shore: A History of Asian Americans*, and the recently published *A Different Mirror: A History of Multicultural America*.

REBECCA STEFOFF is a writer and editor who has published more than 50 nonfiction books for young adults. Many of her books deal with geography and exploration, including the three-volume set *Extraordinary Explorers*, recently published by Oxford University Press. Stefoff also takes an active interest in environmental issues. She served as editorial director for two Chelsea House series—*Peoples and Places of the World* and *Let's Discover Canada*. Stefoff studied English at the University of Pennsylvania, where she taught for three years. She lives in Portland, Oregon.